STRIKES HAVE
FOLLOWED ME
ALL MY LIFE

Emma Mashinini's words as she confronts her own life. There are no words for this achievement – the discipline of creating space and time in this very repressive, stifling atmosphere.

Brigalia Bam
Deputy General Secretary, South African Council of Churches

When the manuscript of this book was put into my hands I began to skim through it. I became totally engrossed and unable to put it down. It is about being a woman.

There is no one who will read unmoved the terrible description of how, while in solitary confinement in prison, Emma Mashinini forgot the name of her own daughter. There is no woman who will not feel the pain of that.

But it is in her description of the daily grinding routine of getting to work early in the morning and home again after dark with the fire to be made, the food to be cooked, the washing and ironing to be done because there are not enough clothes to be able to leave the washing until the weekend, and then when the family is in bed, the cleaning of the house, that Emma Mashinini speaks for women everywhere.

Sheena Duncan
Former President, Black Sash

I met Emma Mashinini when she was staying in Denmark. She came to us because she had been treated so horribly during her imprisonment, and because she was still suffering from the physical and psychological consequences.

In spite of the extremely difficult period that Emma Mashinini had to live through, she still had the strength to show great compassion and humanity towards other people. Her book is saturated with this humanity. It gives a wise and courageous account of her sufferings in jail. Read this book, read how this courageous woman all her life fights for what she feels is right – learn from Emma Mashinini what human dignity means.

Dr Inge Kemp Genefke
Rehabilitation Centre for Torture Victims, Denmark

STRIKES HAVE FOLLOWED ME ALL MY LIFE

Emma Mashinini

A South African Autobiography

Foreword by
Nomalizo
Leah Tutu

Introduction
by Gay W.
Seidman

**ROUTLEDGE
NEW YORK**

Published in 1991 in the U.S.A. and Canada by Routledge
An imprint of Routledge, Chapman and Hall, Inc.
29 West 35 Street
New York, NY 10001

First published in 1989 by The Women's Press, Ltd.
A member of The Namara Group
34 Great Sutton Street
London ECIV ODX

Printed in the United States of America.

Library of Congress Cataloging-in-Publication Data

Mashinini, Emma, 1929-
    Strikes have followed me all my life : a South African autobiography / Emma Mashinini.
        p.   cm.
    ISBN 0-415-90414-5. — ISBN 0-415-90415-3 (pbk.)
    1. Mashinini, Emma, 1929-   . 2. Trade-unions, Black— South Africa—Officials and employees—Biography.
    3. Apartheid—South Africa. 4. Prisions—South Africa.
I. Title.
HD6870.5.Z55M376   1991
322'.2'092—dc20
    [B]   90-22791

None of us was prepared for the full reality of apartheid.

As a contrivance of social engineering, it is awesome in its cruelty. It is achieved and sustained only through force, creating human misery and deprivation and blighting the lives of millions.

Mission to South Africa: the Commonwealth Report –
the Findings of the Eminent Persons Group on Southern Africa,
(1986), p.23

Contents

List of Illustrations x
Foreword by Nomalizo Leah Tutu xi
Acknowledgments xiii
Preface xv
List of Abbreviations xviii
Introduction by Gay W. Seidman xix

Part I

1 Early Years 3
2 Push Your Arse! 13
3 Speaking Back 23
4 Birth of a Union 31
5 A Force to be Reckoned With 41
6 The Arrest of a Commie 49

Part II

7 Pretoria Central Prison 61
8 Jeppe Police Station 71
9 Dudu 79
10 A Kind of Freedom 88
11 Just a Tiny Giant 100
12 Violent Times 115
13 Justice and Reconciliation? 130

Appendix A 136
Appendix B 139

Illustrations

Penny on her fourteenth birthday

Penny with Dudu

Penny at sixteen

Penny's funeral

Molly, with her husband Aubrey and their two children

Emma with her husband Tom and daughter Nomsa on Emma's release from detention, 1982

Mphoentle, Emma's eldest granddaughter

Emma with her daughter Molly and some of the garment workers

Farewell presentation from a branch of the Garment Workers' Union, 1975

Emma with Morris Kagan at the 19th World Congress of FIET, 1979

Emma with members of the Africa Committee of FIET

CCAWUSA Executive Committee

Emma addressing striking workers

Emma with Leah Tutu at a Sharpeville Massacre memorial meeting, 1988

Khotso House after it was bombed

Emma at work in Khotso House as Director of the Department of Justice and Reconciliation of the Church of the Province of South Africa

Emma and Joyce Seroke demonstrating against the visit of Dr Piet Koornhof to Soweto

Foreword by Nomalizo Leah Tutu

In many ways this is a sad book, but it is also a triumphant record of a woman's resilience in the face of men's oppression.

Male domination has indeed followed the writer to her place of work – the boss in the factory, and to her private life – security police who do not respect the sanctity of her bedroom. It follows her to detention without trial – indeed to the bitter end of interrogation intended to break her. Emma does not give in, nor does she give up. She bounces back like a tennis ball to tell her story – the story of a black woman's trials and tribulations in the present day 'Western Standard Democracy' of South Africa.

There is no record of the writer belonging to any unlawful organisation – political or otherwise. She was a trade unionist whose only fight was with unjust employment practices as far as they penalised employees. Therefore rather than the state as such, the employer was her enemy.

In what way then would the state security be endangered by her work? Ask the South African Security Police, who turned her life into the life of a common criminal hounded by police day and night.

Perhaps the fact that she was never brought to appear before a court of law was a proof of her innocence.

The mention of her shiny BMW car and her cut crystal glass may sound strange to foreign ears. But this is a true South African story of black people of the eighties. No right to land, no right to sell your labour where you would – no right to live where you wish, no right to vote. A right to buy the commodities that they produce. Where can we prove that we can be as good as 'they' are? We can drive the same cars and buy the same furniture. One disease common to all true

South Africans, black and white, is the 'see what I have' disease. As blacks it is a form of exorcism – an escape from our dire poverty which has been forced on us by all the restrictive laws. Emma has been bruised but it will take much stronger men and more stringent measures to break this reservoir of black woman power.

Acknowledgments

My grateful thanks and admiration go to my friends and fellow workers in the struggle.

My gratitude goes to my long-suffering family for my prolonged absences from home, this time for something different but fulfilling to me, the writing of this book. Their patience has been inexhaustible and has contributed in making it possible for me to achieve this goal. Without their unfailing support there is little I could do. I think especially of Nomsa, my darling daughter, who lives with me and who has been supportive and shared my agonies and dilemmas; of Dudu, my stimulating and fascinating child, who would always enquire about the progress of the book; of Molly, who was a driving force, and who kept me to my promise to complete this task; of my loving granddaughters Mphoentle (Beautiful Gift) and Rirandzu (Love), who always wished to know if I was mentioning anything about their mom, and who thought that it was very important for the world to know that Molly, their mom, is my daughter.

Sadly, I hate to know that my son-in-law Aubrey Mageza has not lived to share the joy of his mom's book. He, also, was keen to know how the book was progressing. He was extremely proud of my involvement in matters of liberation and was extraordinary in wishing to know about workers' rights. Many of my fellow trade unionists who were studying abroad would visit Molly and Aubrey in Germany, and he was always so thrilled to meet them and so pleased that they were studying in order to return home and run the unions from a position of knowledge of industrial relations and that with that knowledge their bargaining power would be strengthened.

And sadly, again, and finally, I come to my sweetest girl, Penny, who achieved so much before her untimely death at the age of seventeen years.

Preface

Our union, the Commercial, Catering and Allied Workers' Union of South Africa, CCAWUSA, was started under the auspices of the National Union of Distributive Workers, NUDW, in August 1975. Morris Kagan, the chairman of the ad hoc committee, was a strong pillar of support to me at that time, and in the late 1970s, as the union grew from strength to strength, he urged me to write about my role in founding it, and especially to show how, in spite of suffering, our lives are enriched by the struggle to uphold human rights and in the fight for the dignity of individuals.

Bob Plant, the African Desk representative for the International Federation of Commercial, Clerical, Professional and Technical Employees (FIET), based in Geneva, also worked closely with me in those years. He was an expert in trade unionism, and like Morris Kagan was not only an ally in work but also a close personal friend of mine. He, too, encouraged me to write a book about my trade union involvement.

However, I put the idea aside, because I was not sure if doing this at that time would have been of great value, and besides, I was too busy with my union work, which took up all my time.

Strangely enough, it was Bob Plant who first told me of Betty Wolpert, a South African film-maker living in London. He wrote to me in 1981 telling me of a film, *Awake From Mourning*, he would be bringing to our AFRO-FIET meeting in Zimbabwe, representing more than seventeen African countries. Apparently he had searched in London for Betty Wolpert, who produced this film, and asked her to lend him a print. They met the day he flew to Zimbabwe, and she gave him the film, which he showed at that conference. It tells of the courage, dignity and strength of black women in South Africa in the wake of the terrible deaths of the children of Soweto in 1976. I discovered that I knew most of the women in the film, because we had worked together on other projects. Some of them I had worked with at Henochsberg's; others were from nearby factories. These were responsible women who were also shop stewards.

Four years later I finally met Betty. She was staying at the home of a friend of mine, Joyce Seroke, in Soweto. Joyce and Betty were embarking on a new film, called *Mama, I'm Crying*, and they asked me to take part in it. It was during our work on this film that Betty finally persuaded me of the importance of telling my story.

During the shooting of the film, she interviewed me and recorded my story on every possible occasion, even on aeroplane journeys. She would then post the tapes to Ruth Vaughan, her collaborator in London, who would rapidly transcribe them so that I could immediately work on the rough draft. With time I gained confidence and got into the groove of writing chapters myself.

It was Betty who took my manuscript to The Women's Press, and it was at her house in London that I completed the final draft and worked with my editor, Alison Mansbridge. It was lovingly nurtured by her, and she helped to organise my hastily scribbled throughts, which at times were difficult for her to understand because of language differences and my level of education, which to me has never been an embarrassment. As I am not a writer by profession, but rather a speaker, this made her task greater, but she cared deeply about my life and struggle as a black woman in South Africa and put all her energy and her great skills into bringing this book about, and I will be eternally grateful to her.

I would also like to thank Ros de Lanerolle of The Women's Press for so readily accepting my manuscript. She has the honour of still being on the restricted list in South Africa for the part she played in our fight for freedom in the 1950s.

I am very grateful to Joyce Seroke, who was always encouraging and enthusiastic about my book and read my chapters as I went along, coming up with suggestions, and provoking my thinking about many things which she felt I had omitted, and I was thus able to rectify this.

Alan Fine helped with the research for the book. We worked together for some time and I appreciate his support. Dulcie Hartwell gave me useful help with Appendix A on the South African trade union movement.

There were some very painful moments in my past, and also in my present, which I would have liked to forget. There were times when Betty and I were both in tears as I recalled some of these moments, but at the end I must say that putting on paper some of these terrible times was therapeutic, and that if I had my life over again I would willingly follow the same path. Personal tragedies remain painfully with me, but I have no single regret about the part I have played in the struggle for human rights.

I finished writing my final chapter today at 5 a.m. The radio was playing Frank Sinatra singing 'Come Fly With Me', and for that moment I remembered my youthful optimism and excitement, and my romantic expectations of the future, and my spirit soared. I close the manuscript with a surge of elation, hope and happiness.

E.M.
Soweto
3 February 1989

Abbreviations

ANC	African National Congress
BCC	Black Consultative Committee of Trade Unions
CCAWUSA	Commercial, Catering and Allied Workers' Union of South Africa
CNA	Central News Agency
COSATU	Congress of South African Trade Unions
CUSA	Council of Unions of South Africa
DPSC	Detainees' Parents Support Committee
EPG	Eminent Persons Group
FIET	International Federation of Commercial, Clerical, Professional and Technical Employees
FOSATU	Federation of South African Trades Unions
GAWU	General and Allied Workers' Union
GWU	Garment Workers' Union
HOTELICA	Hotel, Liquor and Catering Trade Employees' Union
IUF	International Union of Food and Allied Workers' Associations
NUCAW	National Union of Commercial and Allied Workers
NUDW	National Union of Distributive Workers
PFP	Progressive Federal Party
SAAWU	South African and Allied Workers' Union
SACC	South African Council of Churches
SACTU	South African Congress of Trade Unions
TUCSA	Trade Union Council of South Africa
UTP	Urban Training Project
WPGWU	Western Province General Workers' Union

Introduction by Gay W. Seidman

Emma Mashinini's autobiography is published at a time when South Africa appears on the verge of change. No matter what happens during the next decades, however, Emma's book will continue to be important, for what it teaches about the effects of racial domination, and for what we come to understand about the strength and courage of individuals like Emma Mashinini.

Almost every aspect of Emma's life—like the lives of all South Africans—has been touched by apartheid, the strict racial segregation that has made South Africa notorious. Based on their legal racial classification, apartheid legislation told South Africans where they could live, who they could marry, what schools they could attend, what jobs they could hold. Only the 13.8 percent of the population classified "white" could vote; black South Africans, including Emma Mashinini, were denied political rights in their own country, and attempts to gain those rights risked severe repression from a government determined to protect white-minority rule.*

Like many black South Africans, Emma Mashinini found innumerable ways to challenge a system designed to protect white supremacy, resisting in her daily life the isolation and sense of inferiority that racial domination can create. For black South

---

*Census data in South Africa is highly problematic, but in 1988, the South African Institute of Race Relations estimated the country's population at just under 36 million, divided into the following racial classifications: African—26,974 million (74.9 percent); white—4,949 million (13.8 percent); colored—3,127 million (8.7 percent); Indian—928 thousand (2.6 percent).

Africans, she writes, the first act of politicization is to say, "I am human. I exist. I am a complete person." [p. 24] In all the spheres of her life, Emma has joined other South Africans to fight oppression. In the community created by her family, neighbors and co-workers, she found the strength to continue.

Nevertheless, Emma Mashinini is also unusual. A leading figure in the black trade union movement and in the political struggle against apartheid, her persistent courage has been extraordinary. Having left junior high school to work first as a nanny and later as a textile worker, and while raising her children on her own, in 1975 she became the first national organizer for a fledgling union for black workers in the service sector. Strikes have indeed followed her all her life: the union she helped build has grown into a leading component of South Africa's labor movement, representing millions of working women and men. Since 1985, Emma has monitored the situation of political prisoners for the Anglican Church of the Province of Southern Africa.

By the late 1980s, Emma had become a national political figure, helping to unify resistance and to publicize the government's repression during a prolonged uprising. Despite constant police harassment—including six long months in solitary confinement—she has consistently brought people together to fight for their rights. Like all authors, Emma has chosen her own persona: modesty leads her to emphasize personal experience and group victories, rather than individual accomplishments. But even a slightly understated version of Emma's career adds meaning to the warning black South African women gave the South African government many years ago: "You have tampered with the women. You have struck a rock. You have dislodged a boulder; you will be crushed."[1]

APARTHEID AND RACIAL DOMINATION

To black South Africans, the effects of apartheid are obvious: they can be seen in every aspect of daily life. Thus, Emma Mashinini writes about her life without explaining what apartheid is, how it developed, or how her life has been directly shaped by the laws that maintain racial segregation. She takes these things for granted, as an inevitable part of what it means to be a black South African.* For non-South African readers, however, it is often difficult to accept how overwhelming apartheid's restrictions could be; in the late twentieth century, such extreme forms of racial oppression—which prevented roughly 85 percent of South Africa's 36 million people not classified white from making basic decisions about their lives—appear almost unbelievable. A complete appreciation of the depth of Emma's strength and courage requires first an understanding of what apartheid meant to individuals, and particularly to her, as a black South African, as a woman, and as a worker.

Apartheid is a term including a set of laws and policies enacted by the South African government after 1948—paradoxically, at a time when most of the world was moving away from legalized forms of racial discrimination. The Nationalist Party came to power in a whites-only election, committed to reinforcing the racial domination which had existed since European settlers arrived in South Africa in the 17th century. Many of the laws and institutions on which apartheid was based already existed; but by enforcing racial classification—legally classifying every South African in terms of their racial category at birth, and tying legal and political rights to racial classifications—and

---

*Racial terms in South Africa are constantly changing, and carry different political connotations. Official terminology for people of entirely African descent has changed from "native" to "Bantu" to "black" in just three decades.

South Africans who seek a democratic society argue that racial categories are socially constructed, rather than biological. That fact is underlined in South Africa by the annual official practice of changing some individuals' racial categories—thus completely reshaping their opportunities for employment, education, and, of course, political rights. In 1985, for example, 1,167 South Africans were legally reclassified to a new race group.

Rather than accepting the government's categories, many South Africans since the 1970s have used the term "black" to include people who are officially classified "black" and people classified "Indian" or "Colored," emphasizing unity among the disenfranchised. When referring specifically to government practice, I have tended to differentiate between policy towards South Africans classified African, Indian, and Colored, but in other cases, I have tended to use black.

by enforcing strict segregation throughout society, the government sought to create a society in which the black majority would be permanently subordinated to the demands of the white minority. To protect racial divisions, marriage and intercourse were prohibited between people of different racial categories.

Following the policies of previous white administrations, the Nationalist Party used a racial geography: it set aside only about 13 percent of the country's land area for roughly 75 percent of the population legally classified African. In the 87 percent of South Africa designated for white residence, Africans could not own land or businesses, nor could they move freely. From 1950, over three million Africans would be forced to leave their homes and move onto the overcrowded, poor areas, known as "bantustans" or "homelands," designated for African occupancy. Emma describes visiting her mother-in-law in one of these areas, where the family lived on what they could eke out of the soil. [p. 10]

But the Nationalist Party went further: these homelands were one day to become independent countries, where blacks would be allowed to govern themselves. In the meantime—since they would one day be homeland citizens—blacks were denied citizenship in the rest of their country. Along with geographic separation went segregation of basic political rights: South Africans classified African were expected to view homeland administrators as their representatives, although most homeland leaders were actually appointed by the all-white central government. Denied the right to vote, those who sought non-racial democracy were gradually denied the possibility of any meaningful political expression. Although many South Africans protested vehemently, the government enacted strict security laws, allowing it to jail opponents—including Nelson Mandela—and to outlaw political parties which challenged white domination, including Mandela's African National Congress and the Pan-Africanist Congress.

Like thousands of other South Africans who fought apartheid, when Emma was detained in 1981, she was never brought to trial. Although she suspects the security police may have thought a plan to build a workers' center was linked to underground activities of the outlawed African National Congress [p. 50], she will probably never be sure why she was detained. And even at the time of this writing, when South Africa appears on the brink of change, Emma—like most of her country's population—cannot vote, simply because she is black.

Nevertheless, despite legal segregation and racial oppression, white South Africa was never deprived of black labor. Apartheid planners recognized that black workers were essential for white-owned farms, industries, and in the mines on which the country's wealth was based. Without black workers, the economy would have collapsed. Although people classified African were expected to make their homes inside bantustan borders, those who could provide labor to white-owned enterprises were given passes to stay in white-designated South Africa for as long as they remained useful, while those officially considered "nonproductive" were sent away to rural areas. As a government circular put it in 1967:

> It is accepted government policy that [Africans] are only temporarily resident in the European areas of the Republic, for as long as they offer their labor there. As soon as they become, for one reason or another, no longer fit for work or superfluous in the labor market, they are expected to return to [the homeland] where they fit in ethnically if they were not born and bred in the homeland.[2]

Until 1986, people over 16 who were classified African were required to carry their passes at all times, and at least 12.5 million people were arrested for breaking pass laws between 1948 and 1981. Emma describes seeing her 17-year-old daughter Penny on her way to get her pass in order; [p. 128] without the correct documents, Penny risked being sentenced to either a fine, forcible removal to a homeland, or three months' labor on a white-owned farm.

Even those black South Africans who, like Emma, had permission to work and live in white-designated areas could not move about freely: blacks were forced to move to separate areas on the edges of towns. A major motivation for the tightening of racial segregation in the early 1950s was the growth of the urban black population; after World War II, black resistance was more visible than it had ever been, and the white-minority government sought new ways to control the country's majority. Through the late 1940s and early 1950s, black South Africans organized strikes, boycotts, and civil disobedience campaigns. Apartheid was designed in part to end these disturbances, by reinforcing segregation and state control, especially in urban centers.[3]

Under Nationalist Party policies, whites would live in city centers, where most commerce and industry was located. People classified in other racial groups would live outside town, coming into town only to work. People classified African would live in one residential area, or township; those classified Indian (descendants of immigrants from India) or Colored (mixed-race) in others. The 1950 Group Areas Act—still in effect at the time of this writing—led the police to bulldoze vibrant, racially-mixed neighborhoods, as the government forced people to move into artificially-created segregated areas. One of the most famous removals was that of Johannesburg's Sophiatown, where Emma grew up. [p. 4] Residents classified African were forced to move to Soweto, where at first there was almost nothing: no electricity, no running water, no paved roads, no shops, no parks, with long commutes (in Emma's case, 30 kilometers [p. 14]), and, perhaps worst of all, with little of the urban community which might have strengthened resistance to apartheid.[4] As Emma remarks, the all-white suburb which replaced Sophiatown was given a telling name: Triomf, meaning "Triumph."

The effect of white-minority rule has been to distort the distribution of South Africa's wealth, so that nearly all the country's extraordinary resources went to the small minority classified white. Emma describes the effects of these policies on the lives of her family through graphic examples. Lacking basic medical attention, three of her babies died of an easily curable disease. [p. 8] She battled to pay school fees for her surviving children [p. 27]—who, if they had been classified white, would have gone for free to whites-only schools offering a decent education. Instead, they struggled through their schoolwork by candlelight [p. 16], forced by strict segregation to attend underfunded, under-equipped schools, with curricula explicitly designed to teach them "from childhood . . . that equality with Europeans is not for them."[5] Since the 1976 Soweto student uprising [p. 20], in which hundreds of black children were killed in their protest against inferior education, black students have been extremely active in the struggle against apartheid. Without adequate training, these students have been denied skills needed for a rapidly-industrializing economy.

These two examples—the lack of health care and educational facilities—are only two of the multiple ways a government geared to serve the white minority has blocked black South Africans' access to basic social services. Health, education, housing shortages [p. 123], and the lack of public transport [p. 39] are among the most severe deprivations, but apartheid will leave a bitter legacy: a democratically-elected government will have to find ways to resolve basic needs, and to overcome a long history of state discrimination.

Emma describes the psychological effects of racial domination, especially the sense of inferiority that can be instilled by a social structure designed to protect white supremacy. The use of dangerous skin-lightening creams [p. 9] or the decision to spend scarce household money to look fashionable [p. 11] are only two symptoms of a diseased society, in which people have internalized oppression.

But for foreign readers, perhaps even more striking is the degree to which Emma, like many black South Africans, insists on her own human dignity, and that of her neighbors and fellow workers. When she speaks of her community—of the many people with whom she has lived and worked, from her neighbors to mothers of prisoners on death row [p. 134], from workers greeting white employers as equals [p. 102] to her husband bravely demonstrating against her imprisonment [p. 81]—Emma joyfully acknowledges the strength of the human spirit. In the solidarity found in resisting oppression, she writes, "Your problem is never your problem alone, you are never an island in your problem . . . We unite, and especially we unite in our crisis times." [p. 134]

Like many black South African activists, however, Emma is also willing to extend this sense of community to whites who have joined the struggle against racial domination and minority rule. When she writes lovingly of white colleagues in the trade union movement or the church [p. 32 and 104], she does so not from a sense of inferiority, but with respect, because despite their upbringing within the white minority, they, too, have sought to bring people together to challenge white supremacy. Racism has affected all South Africans, although in different ways. Emma writes, "Segregation, the setting of one off against another—this breeds a corruption from which none of us, whatever our color, can be free." [p. 118] To Emma, all those who work for change, whatever their background or legal racial classification, offer hope for a future democratic South Africa, in which people will be viewed as individuals, not as members of racial categories.

APARTHEID AND GENDER

One of the most poignant moments of Emma Mashinini's autobiography is when she describes a painful time in solitary confinement when she could not remember her youngest daughter's name. [p. 86] The depth of this despair, the sense of total isolation and misery, are unmistakable; and in the South African context, it is no small measure of Emma's courage that she is willing to describe what appears to have been a spell of clinical depression in prison, and a virtual nervous breakdown on her release. As she says, South Africans have tended to attach some stigma to psychotherapy of any sort. [p. 113] In a decades-long struggle which has demanded real sacrifices—in which activists regularly confront arrest, exile, torture, even death—it is often considered a sign of weakness to admit that under pressure, one lost courage. But as Emma says, rather than seeing such moments as weakness, it is better to remember them, to tell one's children: the psychological trauma wrought by fear and repression on millions of oppressed South Africans, women and men, becomes itself "a living memory of the evil of the apartheid regime." [p. 110]

This moment, however, is also a reminder that Emma Mashinini is a mother, who, as a woman, experienced apartheid slightly differently than the men around her. One of the more vicious aspects of the pass system is that while men receive permission to seek work in white-designated towns, their wives, children, and the aged are often left in rural bantustans, dependent on subsistence agriculture and on money sent back by migrant workers. For many families the strain has proved overwhelming. Many African women have been left raising children on their own, as marriage loses any real meaning. As a child, Emma's mother was the only parent in her life. When she left her husband, in part because of the strains of poverty and hard work, Emma, too, became a single mother. Emma herself was lucky enough to have had the legal pass needed to remain in Soweto and to keep her children together after the divorce; but her experience as a single mother is probably far more common than her later experience with a second, supportive husband.

Gender patterns—including both traditional family patterns which assign most household responsibilities to women, and government laws that treat women as legal minors, dependent on their husbands—combine with race and poverty to put enormous obstacles in front of African women. In an example that is all too common, Emma describes her difficulties buying a car; unwilling to buy it in her husband's name, she was refused credit. [p. 94] The circumstances under which she was able to collect the down payment for her car [p. 99], like those of its final destiny [p. 122], are uniquely Emma's, linked to her long political involvement and to the history of South African government repression; but the problems she had in dealing with a system which assumes women are dependent and incompetent are common to women all over her country.

Emma is by no means alone in challenging gender ideologies. Many South African women have gone far beyond traditional expectations. To overlook the extent to which she, like every woman in South Africa, has had to fight gender discrimination would be to ignore the degree to which black South African women face different expectations and responsibilities than their brothers. Women all over the world confront a double shift, with responsibilities at home and at work. But black South African women, as Emma points out, face additional burdens caused by extremely low wages for both women and men, and problems caused by the high percentage of female-headed households which is largely related, in turn, to the effects of the migrant labor system. Emma writes from personal experience of how women end up with primary responsibility for both earning an income and for raising children.

There is no need to discuss here the ways in which black South African women support each other: throughout her book, although she never uses the word feminist, Emma describes how the women of her community help each other get through difficult times. The community-based informal groups, such as the *stokvels* through which women raise funds for each other [p. 17], may be different in content from the more political women's organizations to which Emma belonged [p. 82], but the basic idea remains the same. Like millions of other South African women, Emma has regularly joined other women in autonomous networks and organizations through which they help themselves and each other. From her mother-in-law, to the daughters of whom she is so proud, to other political activists with whom she works, Emma readily acknowledges how much she has depended on women throughout her life.

But as a trade unionist, Emma gives special attention to the problems of working women. Emma worked because her family could not live on what her husband earned, and she was, as she recognized, lucky to find a job at all, in one of the few industries that would hire black women in the 1950s. [p. 13] Since then, however, more and more African women have been hired in industrial and service sector jobs; employers often believe that women make more docile workers, and until 1981 the government allowed employers to pay women workers lower wages than men. By 1985, women made up about a third of the paid workforce, although most worked in low-paid jobs in the food, clothing, and textile industries, the service sector, and as farm laborers. Many black women could not find regular jobs, and worked instead in what is sometimes called the informal sector, selling goods in open-air markets to survive.[6]

Emma's union, the Commercial, Catering and Allied Workers Union of South Africa, CCAWUSA (later renamed the South African Commercial, Catering and Allied Workers Union, SAC-CAWU) represents a sector that is increasingly female, as black women workers are hired to work as cleaners and cashiers, and in food preparation. In 1985, when Emma retired from the union, four-fifths of all service workers were black. Sixty percent of her union members were women. [p. 118] Her union work brought her into daily contact with the problems facing working women. When she says that unions must be involved in every aspect of workers' lives, her belief that this includes "the whole question of equality between men and women" [p. 119] stems from lived reality.

Emma dwells on some of the indignities faced by the women she represented [p. 114], but she is far more modest about the real breakthroughs her union has made. In 1983, while Emma was still with the union, CCAWUSA became the first black union to win a contract giving women workers paid maternity leave, guaranteeing they could return to their jobs. [p. 117] Since then, maternity benefits have been included in more and more contracts. Unions which represent large percentages of women have become increasingly likely to include issues in contract negotiations that reflect the special needs of working women: equal pay for work of equal value, an end to gender-based discrimination in hiring and promotions, child care facilities, the right to take off time to care for sick children, and an end to sexual harassment on the job.[7]

Nevertheless, as Emma herself points out, even her own union still has some way to go to represent women's needs fully. In 1990, five years after Emma retired from the union, although most of her union's members were women, union officers were nearly all men. Union organizers explained that it was often difficult for women workers to participate in union activities, both because their family responsibilities keep them busy and because gender ideologies tend to keep women silent at mixed meetings.[8] Along with the rest of a small group of women who are nationally-recognized activists, Emma is widely-respected by other working women, who see her independence and energy as a model for women throughout the community.

APARTHEID AND LABOR CONTROL

Apartheid is a system of racial domination, and it is a system under which black women and men experience different kinds of oppression. But apartheid is also a system of labor control. Especially from the late nineteenth century, when European companies began to open South Africa's mines, the issue of how to create, maintain, and control a black labor force dominated white political discussions: the pass laws, along with the system of what became homelands, evolved through the early 20th century, as white mineowners, farmers, and industrialists sought to ensure a steady supply of black workers who could not organize to demand higher wages.[9] Johannesburg, where Emma Mashinini spent most of her life, is built on top of some of the world's richest mineral deposits; since the late 19th century, South Africa has been a major source of the world's gold, diamonds, uranium and other metals. But without cheap labor, the mines would not have been profitable; without cheap labor, white-owned farms would not have been so productive. The apartheid system gave employers enormous power over the lives of individual workers. Even in the late 1970s, when industrial growth meant that black workers were increasingly engaged in semi-skilled work and could not easily be fired and replaced, employers continued to use apartheid legislation to prevent workers from organizing at the workplace to demand higher wages.

For most of Emma's working life, black workers had virtually no rights at the workplace: no right to organize unions, no right to strike, no right to protection from arbitrary dismissal. Individual workers who challenged employer authority were frequently fired, and, with the loss of their job, faced the loss of their pass to live in urban areas. In 1980, Emma's union protested when the government sent 12,000 striking municipal workers out of Johannesburg to the rural homelands to which apartheid restricted non-working Africans. [p. 48] Workers who tried to form unions risked being labelled political agitators. Unions representing black workers could not enter into legal negotiations with employers. Emma was lucky to have begun work in a textile factory, where a legal union had created separate "parallel" branches for workers of different racial classifications. But even in this case, the union could not negotiate for its black members. Wages for black workers were set by national councils controlled by the white-minority government and employers. [p. 18][10]

Nor could black workers look for help from most white unionists. From the early 20th century, most white labor leaders supported strict racial divisions at the workplace, and tried to prevent black workers from entering training programs or moving into more skilled jobs. From the early 1920s, white labor leaders excluded black workers from their unions, and insisted that jobs above certain levels of pay and skill be set aside for whites—leaving only less-skilled, lower-paid jobs for blacks. As apartheid was tightened in the 1950s, the government gradually strengthened these "job reservation" policies, keeping workplaces segregated and preventing black mobility within factories and mines. [p. 20][11] The long history of the color bar—which was only legally removed in the mid-1970s, when employers complained bitterly about shortages of white workers for skilled positions in a growing industrial economy, but which continues to operate unofficially in many South African companies—makes Emma's promotion to supervisor [p. 18] even more unusual, and helps explain her distrust of her employers' motives.

In 1975, when Emma was asked to help organize CCAWUSA, the South African trade union movement was going through an unusual resurgence. In 1973, more than 100,000 African workers across South Africa had gone on strike for higher wages and union representation. The sudden strikewave took employers and the government by surprise. Black industrial workers demonstrated that they could use their own shopfloor organizations to win improvements in wages and working conditions. Over the next few years, despite severe repression, black workers gradually formed their own trade unions. In 1979, faced with persistent labor activism and international pressure, the government changed its labor legislation to give black workers the right to organize legally-recognized unions and to negotiate with employers. [p. 43][12]

By the time Emma left the labor movement to work for the Church of the Province of Southern Africa, the South African labor movement had become a force which neither employers or the state could ignore. But for most of the decade she worked for CCAWUSA, she faced constant harassment and danger. When she began her union work, black activists—including both workers and union officials—could never be sure when they might be arrested without charges, tortured, even killed. Working closely with employers, the South African security police

constantly watched trade unionists for any hint of illegal political activity. As Emma writes, "In our industrial relations in South
Africa you deal not only with the employers when you negotiate but you deal with the police as well." [p. 75] The fledgling
unions had no legal protection and few resources, not even office furniture. Workers who joined were often fired, and when
there were strikes, the unions had no strike funds to help workers' families survive weeks without pay—families who were
struggling to survive even before the strike. It is an extraordinary tribute to the courage of working South Africans, and, above
all, to the courage and persistence of organizers like Emma, that
the South African labor movement survived and flourished to
the point where today, it is one of the strongest and most militant in the world.

Emma's perspective on trade unionism in a racially-divided
society is complex. Should unions try to represent all workers
of any racial category, or should their organization reflect the
racial stratification of the society in which they operate? On one
hand, Emma expresses real gratitude to white unionists who
assisted her early efforts in forming CCAWUSA [p. 31–2], ap-
plauds her union's decision to strike in support of a demoted
white worker, [p. 117] and describes her horror and anger at
the death in detention of a white unionist dedicated to organizing black workers. [p. 80–1] On the other, she insists that
under apartheid, African workers face very different problems
than workers in other racial categories, because of the government's refusal to provide basic services to people classified African. [p. 39] CCAWUSA initially represented only African workers, although it worked closely with another union representing
shopworkers classified Indian or Colored; [p. 30] in 1979, CCA-
WUSA refused to join a united labor federation because its
members feared the organization would be dominated by white
intellectuals. [p. 33]

In fact, the two positions are not inconsistent: Emma supported worker solidarity, but she also believed that African
workers had to represent themselves, to gain the confidence
and organizational strength needed to ensure that their voices
would be heard. As the labor movement grew, and as employers
were forced to recognize and negotiate with black unions, Emma

watched union members begin to say, "We are not slaves. We are workers." [p. 45] As they experienced successful strikes, organized community support and consumer boycotts in support of striking workers, [p. 47] and stood up to the employers who once intimidated them, [p. 101] black workers learned to articulate demands and lead their own organizations.

By 1985, when CCAWUSA joined the Congress of South African Trade Unions—which includes workers of all racial categories, though most of its members are black—Emma could feel confident that the labor movement would not focus simply on workplace issues, or that more educated, more privileged workers would speak for African workers. The labor movement she helped create would take up all the problems facing its members, including black workers' lack of political rights and unequal access to public resources. She writes:

> The trade union movement is a very powerful organisation, and it is not there just to look at the bread and butter problems of workers. The trade union movement is concerned with the liberation of the people in South Africa. Because if the trade union organization cannot take on the issue of the liberation of the country, who will? . . . The trade unions have got to follow the workers in all their travels—to get them home, and to school, in the education and welfare of their children, everywhere. The whole life of a worker needs trade union involvement. [p. 119]

Today, as the country appears to be moving toward a nonracial democracy, no one in South Africa doubts that the labor movement which Emma helped to build will fight to improve all aspects of workers' lives, both inside the factory and beyond its gates, or that the labor movement will play a key role in shaping the country's future.

FOR HUMAN DIGNITY

Emma wrote her autobiography before Mandela and other political prisoners were released, before the African National Congress and other political parties were unbanned, at a moment when what she calls "the day of liberation" [p. 135] still seemed far away. Only two years later, the future appears much closer, as Mandela and other leaders negotiate with the white-minority government over how to create a democratically-elected government that will treat all South Africans as equals.

It will be decades before the legacy of apartheid disappears. Such a divided society, in which the country's majority has been systematically denied access to jobs, education, health care, and property, is a society in which violence has long been systemic. Emma's family's experience warns her of the dangers; she writes, "In such an area of despair, paranoia and hatred can easily be inflamed." [p. 124] Emma's book bears witness to the evil of apartheid, as she meant it to do. Yet her autobiography also bears witness to the promise of South Africa. Together with millions of other South Africans, Emma refused to abandon a vision of a just, peaceful society, in which all the people of her country would be free. Of her efforts to bring people together to speak for themselves, Emma writes:

> It was vital that we should be recognised for who we were, and that we should fight for our identity and respect as human beings. That was the battle we had to fight then. And human dignity is the battle we must still fight. [p. 40]

Reading this book, no one could doubt the outcome: the struggle for human dignity is one from which Emma Mashinini has already emerged, victorious.

October, 1990.

NOTES

1. Sung during the 1956 anti-pass campaign, described in Cherryl Walker, *Women and Resistance in South Africa* (London: Onyx Press, 1982), pp. 189–201.

2. The Secretary for Bantu Administration and Development, General Circular no. 25, 1967; reprinted in International Defense and Aid Fund for Southern Africa, *Apartheid: the Facts* (London: IDAF, 1983), p. 20.

3. Harold Wolpe, "Capitalism and Cheap Labour-Power in South Africa: From Segregation to Apartheid," *Economy and Society* 111:4 (1972), p. 425–456.

4. For descriptions of urban struggles against removals, see Tom Lodge, *Black Politics in South Africa Since 1945* (Johannesburg: Ravan Press, 1983), especially chapters 3–7.

5. Minister of Native Affairs Hendrik Verwoerd in parliament, introducing a 1953 law to reform education for Africans; quoted in Neil Parsons, *A New History of South Africa* (London: Macmillan Education Ltd, 1982), p. 292. For the effects of apartheid on education, see William Finnegan's *Crossing the Line: A Year in the Land of Apartheid* (New York: Harper and Row, 1986).

6. Moira Maconachie, "Looking for Patterns of Women's Employment and Educational Achievement in the 1985 Census," *Agenda* 5 (1989), 80–92.

7. Barbara Klugman, "Women Workers in the Unions," *South African Labour Bulletin* 14:4 (1989), 13–35.

8. SACCAWU organizers interviewed in Johannesburg, July 1990.

9. Stanley Greenberg, *Race and State in Capitalist Development* (Berkeley: University of California Press, 1980).

10. For histories of the South African trade union movement before the 1970s, see: Ken Luckhard and Brenda Wall, *Organize or Starve* (London: Lawrence and Wishart, 1980); Don Ncube, *The Influence of Apartheid and Capitalism on the Development of Black Trade Unions in South Africa* (Johannesburg: Skotaville Press, 1985); and Eddie Webster (ed.), *Essays in Southern African Labour History* (Johannesburg: Ravan Press, 1978).

11. Eddie Webster, *Cast in a Racial Mould: Labour Process and Trade Unionism in the Foundries* (Johannesburg: Ravan Press, 1985). For a debate about white workers' organizations and apartheid, see Edna Bonacich, "Capitalism and Race Relations in South Africa: A Split Labor Market Analysis," and Michael Burawoy, "The Capitalist State in South Africa: Sociological Perspectives on Race and Class," both in *Political Power and Social Theory* 2 (1981), 239–343.

12. Steven Friedman, *Building Tomorrow Today: African Workers in Trade Unions, 1970–1984* (Johannesburg: Ravan Press, 1987); Johann Maree (ed.), *The Independent Trade Unions, 1974–1984* (Johannesburg: Ravan Press, 1987); Jeremy Baskin, *History of COSATU,* forthcoming.

I

1

Early Years

I was born on 21 August 1929 at 18 Diagonal Street, Rosettenville, a white suburb in southern Johannesburg. My mother, Joana, although to my knowledge she had never been a domestic worker, did some housework in order to pay for our accommodation. We lived in the back yard. My father, Elias Mhlolo Ngwenya, was working for a dairy and had to start out at dawn, so we didn't see much of him at the time. I was the third child of a big family, with six sisters and a brother. My elder sister, Beauty, died at a young age and was buried in the Brixton cemetery, which was later to become exclusively for whites. Even our cemeteries became segregated.

When I was six years old we moved to Prospect Township, in City Deep, south-east of Johannesburg. My mother became a dressmaker of repute, sewing clothes for people in the community, and since both my parents were working very hard and doing quite well for themselves we children started school early – that is, at what would be the normal age for white children. We also went to the better schools available, since although my parents had never received much in the way of formal education, they did everything to ensure their children did. For this I remain very grateful.

So I attended the City Deep Methodist school in Heidelberg Road, Johannesburg, until 1936, when we suffered our first forced removal to make way for a white suburb. I was too young to remember much of our time there, but I do recall our home. My mother sold milk, supplied by our father, from the *stoep* (veranda), and although it was only a one-bedroomed house we somehow managed to live comfortably there. We were happy in our home.

We could have moved to Orlando, which is now part of Soweto, but my parents chose instead to go to Sophiatown, which in those days was a racially mixed area, apart from whites, with many African, Indian and Chinese families all living harmoniously together. Our home was in Toby Street. On the corner of Toby and Edward Street lived a distinguished black doctor, Dr Xuma, one-time President of the African National Congress, who was married to a black American who was responsible for founding the YWCA centre in Soweto. Sophiatown was owned by Sol Tobiansky, who named it after his wife Sophia, and some of the streets after his children, Toby, Bertha, Gerty and Edith. Toby Street was the first street of Sophiatown. Just across a vacant field from us was the white suburb of Westdene. The field was there to divide us, but black and white children used to meet there regularly and play with one another. It seemed the most natural thing to do.

That vibrant community of Sophiatown also disappeared, a few years later, when Sophiatown was declared a white area. The whole population passively resisted and was forcibly and mercilessly crushed by 2,500 police and soldiers. That ill-fated population was moved out of sight and put in Meadowlands, fifteen to twenty miles away, out of sight of Johannesburg. But the home of Dr Xuma still stands as a silent witness to this outrage.

The whites gloatingly re-christened Sophiatown and called it Triomf (Triumph), but Don Mattera, our black South African poet, who lived in Sophiatown, wrote:

> Memory is a weapon. I knew deep down inside of me, in that place where laws and guns cannot reach nor jackboots trample, that there had been no defeat. In another day, another time, we would emerge to reclaim our dignity and our land. It was only a matter of time and Sophiatown would be reborn.

From Sophiatown I was now sent to a Salvation Army school in the municipal Western Native Township nearby, where I discovered how few of my classmates had started school at the correct age. My family was fortunate in other ways, too. I don't remember any of us running around without shoes, and I had a raincoat, unlike many of the children, although since I was sickly in those days I knew that whenever it rained I'd get tonsillitis anyway, and be unable to go to school.

After Standard Six I went on to the Bantu High School in Western Native Township, which was headed by Mr Madibane, whilst my eldest sister, Elizabeth, was at St Peter's Anglican Boarding/ Secondary school in Rosettenville, which was a far superior school. But my family could not afford two children at boarding school.

The memory of our little house in Toby Street always fills me with happiness, and with gratitude to my mother for creating such a home for us. Our home was so welcoming that from every school I attended our teachers would follow us there and become family friends.

There was one room and a kitchen. That was all. This one room served as a dining room and a bedroom, and in order for my parents to have some privacy they erected a curtain separating their bed from the rest of the room. Six of us slept on the other side of this curtain, on the floor, with thick blankets as mattresses. The kitchen had room for a table and two long wooden benches which were scrubbed daily, and we had a black coal stove which stood shining in its corner. On our kitchen dresser hung blue Delft china cups, and on the dresser were crystal glasses and shining brass vases. From my childhood and because of my mother I grew to love beautiful things.

Of course, we had no bathroom or running water in the house, but there was a tap in the yard, and we used a tin tub to bathe in. When it was raining, because of my tonsillitis, my mother would not allow me to wash myself but lovingly would rub me down. She made all our clothes, and again because of my tonsillitis she would make mine from a warmer material. My petticoats were of striped flannelette.

I am the only child of my mother to have inherited her dark skin colour, and I have her identical features. I love to dress well, also, and when I think of my mother I always remember how when she went to town she would wear gloves and high-heeled shoes, and how she would always return holding a bunch of flowers and a cake. She was also extremely strict. If we had visitors and we children were fidgeting she didn't have to say anything. One look was sufficient! She would never allow us to go barefoot, either. We always wore socks and shoes. Amongst poor people this was a particular pride.

And there was music in that home. In the bedroom/dining room we had an organ, and on this my younger sister would play hymns. There was a wind-up HMV gramophone on which my mother would play her Columbia records of African choral music. But what I remember with utmost joy was the front *stoep*. This was of red polished cement, glittering around the straw mat in the centre, with two half-cut paraffin tins painted a bright green and filled with the plants my mother always called 'elephant's ears' but which today I know as rubber plants, one on either side, while on each side of the front door stood a large half-drum, also painted bright green, and filled with 'Xmas' plants (hydrangeas) which flowered pink and blue, in December, in the height of our summer. And in the middle of our *stoep*, in a hanging cage, was a singing yellow canary.

The happiness of this home was shattered for me when my parents separated. This came as a terrible shock to me, even though we weren't seeing much of my father at the time, since he was still working for the same dairy as before, seven days a week, and since he was provided with living quarters he would return home only once a week. Even then he would return home late at night and leave around three in the morning to cycle back to work.

But when my father disappeared now, completely, my family broke up. My mother and youngest sister went to live in Cape Town with an elder sister, while my brother and my other sisters went to Volksrust, the town where my mother was born, on the old road about halfway between Johannesburg and Durban, to stay with our grandparents. I, at the age of about fifteen, was the only one who decided to stay near Johannesburg, and try to find my father.

Due to the break-up of my parents' marriage our funds deteriorated and I was forced to leave school before completing my Junior certificate. I had tried very hard to remain at school, and would baby-sit for white children in the suburbs after school was over, earning three rand per month, but finally I had no alternative but to leave. Even then I would not give up my search for my father. I was determined to find him, and I did eventually manage to track him down with the help of the dairy owner, whose son, a building contractor in Florida, west of Johannesburg, my father was now working for. When I visited my father he said he'd visit me in

Alexandra, where I was staying with an aunt. He never did. The next time I saw him was after another search, a year and a half later, by which time he had moved to Pretoria. He kept on making commitments, but he never followed them up. I think that was my first fight for human rights, my own right to have a father.

When eventually he came to live in Alexandra I was already starting to work on my own, cleaning, and I visited him regularly. But my education was over, and perhaps that was one of the reasons I married so young, at the age of seventeen: I had no school to go to, and no stable home of my own. But I am proud I didn't have to get married. The children came afterwards.

Although he hadn't been the perfect parent, I loved my father dearly. For one thing, as an old man he was very good-natured, and a good grandfather. Despite his age, he continued to build new rooms on to his house for my family to stay in, in case they should ever need to. And although he didn't provide a home and shelter for me when I was young and most needed it, I stayed with him for a long time when my first marriage broke up. He gave me comfort then. I suppose he must have known I didn't hold any grudge against him for leaving us when he did and for his many years of neglect, and perhaps he appreciated that, and that was why we remained so close. We had a long and good relationship, and he was a pillar of strength to my family and a central figure to all his neighbours, supporting himself until his last day on the pension he received from a German company, where he had been a general worker.

My father understood what kind of work I did, and appreciated it. The only time there was any debate was when I was released from detention and he said, 'Don't you think it's time to stop?' But my brother said, 'No. It's not the right time. It would be like giving in to them, or selling out.' We ended by saying, 'Just one more year.' But one year became two, and eventually four. My father was concerned for me, but never ashamed. He knew I never committed any crime.

He died in October 1987, at the age of eighty-seven.

My mother had died twenty-seven years before, at the age of fifty-one, having suffered from high blood pressure. She also died in October. Her grave is in Muizenberg, Cape Town.

I married in 1947, and then I stayed at home. I was a housewife. My first child was born in 1949, and thereafter I had another baby in

1951, and another in 1952, and another in 1954, so it was just babies, babies, all the time. My last baby was born in 1956. I bore six in all, but three died within days of their birth. I didn't know at the time what had caused their deaths, although I can see now it must have been yellow jaundice. Then, in my ignorance, I didn't see that anything was wrong with them. At that time black people wanted their skin to be lighter. Those children seemed to me beautiful, with their lovely light yellow complexions. And the jaundice was never diagnosed.

It might surprise some people that I could lose three babies, each time soon after birth, and not know the cause. But it is typical of white doctors working in our black hospitals to treat patients, and cram them with pills and mixtures, without ever telling them the cause of their illness. Even when you are brave enough to ask, the doctor gets irritable and asks you not to waste his time. I don't know whether it's because our hospitals are overcrowded and therefore the doctors cannot cope with the workload; or whether they think they are doing us a favour because black doctors are few, and so we should be grateful and shut up. To me, on the contrary, it seems that we are doing them a favour, because all our hospitals are training hospitals attached to their medical schools, and with all the peculiar diseases we suffer from, we make excellent guinea-pigs. Sadly, though, some of our own black nurses have fallen victim to this bad habit of not discussing the patient's illness and are spiteful when you ask what is wrong with you. They have even coined a word for a patient who wants information: they call her '*i Graju*', meaning you are a graduate, too educated for your own good.

I remember when the first of my children died. The nurse came from the clinic to wash the baby and so forth. I think it was the third day or so that she'd visited, and she said we must go to the clinic. I asked why, and then thought it must be something to do with the baby's extra finger, which they'd tied off, to cut off the circulation.

When we got to the clinic we were taken by ambulance to Baragwanath. I was holding this lovely baby of mine – she was very plump, and everybody was taking her hand saying, 'Look at this lovely baby.' I wasn't the only one who thought she was beautiful. Then the doctors took her and examined her, and said they had to rush her to the ward. And when I got to the ward, that lovely yellow baby of mine had turned almost blue, and no one told me why.

There was a drip, and I was upset, and I remember my husband had come looking for me – and the next thing the baby was dead. That beautiful yellow baby.

This thinking that anything that is light-skinned is beautiful has caused so much harm. I don't think anyone escaped it. I myself used skin lighteners when I was working, but I'm one of the lucky people who didn't get cancer from them.[1] Most of my people have damaged skins, just because we thought that if we were light we'd have the same privileges as the whites. When you're working side by side with someone with a lighter skin in a factory and you find they're given preference, it's hard not to believe a lighter skin is better for you. Now black consciousness has saved us from hating the colour of our skin. We used to wear wigs, too, to help give the appearance of being fair, and we used to have terrible struggles with our own hair, to make it straighter. And when we had our photographs taken the negatives would be lightened for us, to make us look as much like white people as possible. I have a photograph of myself wearing my wig, and it saddens me. Even then, looking at my face, I don't think that wig made me too happy.

The only thing we still have a quarrel with, even today, is our weight, and that we continue to fight against, because to be overweight is bad for our health. We know it is the food we eat that is to blame, and that the cheapest food is the most fattening food, and the least nutritious. So we can fight this problem with pride, because we want to be healthy and to look good as people – not as white

[1] In the late 1960s black women in South Africa, especially the ill-educated, started using skin lighteners, mainly to compete with the fair-skinned, so-called 'coloured', women who have better status socially and at work. Little did they know that hydroquinin, the chemical present in these creams, has been held responsible for untold harm when used on the face. Thousands of black women have been treated by skin specialists, and some who have developed skin cancer cannot be cured. For many years, professional organisations like the Dermatological Association of South Africa have been fighting for a total ban on hydroquinin in skin-lightening creams. This matter was further taken up by the National Black Consumers' Union and other concerned women's organisations in the country. But the authorities are not prepared to ban hydroquinin, and the draft Bill which was gazetted on 20 May 1988 to ban this harmful ingredient has now been shelved. The Minister of National Health and Population Development, Dr Dawie van Niekerk, decided to give the manufacturers of these creams another three years' grace to stop marketing these products.

people. Many young black people are very slim, including my own children. They take exercise, where we just worked and didn't have enough money for food, let alone sport.

When I met my first husband, Roger, I thought he was very nice because he was handsome and he used to dress well. And when he chose me to be his wife I was proud, because he had chosen me from all the women he could have had.

It was the tradition then that a newly married woman should spend much of her time staying with her in-laws, on her own. It was a point of pride to be able to say, 'I am well accepted. My in-laws love me.' If your husband sent money to you, he didn't have to send it to you as his wife, but would send it to his mother, who would tell you, or not tell you. I was lucky with my mother-in-law, who lived in a rural area in what was once known as Mafeking.[1] She would pass everything he sent on to me, and although she wasn't working, she was ploughing and had some stock cattle and so on, so we lived from all that she could get as produce. I went to live with her when I had Molly, and I lived quite well there.

Then I went back to my husband and brought up our children in our one-roomed house in Kliptown. We lived behind the landlord's cottage, in one of the rooms at the back of the yard. There were three houses like ours facing the front, and three facing almost the back, and ours was a corner room facing the back. A fence divided one house from the other. I had a bed and a wardrobe, and I'd put empty apple boxes one on top of another. In the bottom one I'd store my pots, and in the top one the plates and cups, and on top of these boxes I'd put the two water buckets, and a pot and kettle, which were all aluminium. We had a small black stove in the corner, and two benches and a table.

I would spend the whole day at that table. There were the nappies to be changed, and the children and myself to feed, and then I'd clean those buckets and the pot and kettle with Brasso or whatever until they glittered like mirrors. And I'd polish the black stove, and scrub the benches and the tables. Cleanliness, you see, was another matter of pride among us. We polished in order to keep some self-respect, because the conditions we lived in were so terrible.

[1] Mafeking has since been included in the so-called homeland of Bophutaswana. It is now known as Mabatho and is the capital of Bophutaswana.

I was fortunate that in the yard where I was living there was a well. The others had to come to this same well, and some people had to travel a long way for water. Then came a time when we were told we shouldn't drink the water, as it was polluted, but should use it only for household and laundry work. So I would put my glittering bucket on my head and travel a long way to another well to draw water, but we could never be sure that that well was clean, and whether the person doing the inspection was reliable. Looking back, I realise how often my children were ill, and wonder about that water. And of course the toilets were also in the yard, and they weren't drained properly but were really just another well. They smelled very bad.

To my disappointment, within five years I had to admit that my marriage was no longer what it had been. There were just too many quarrels. Always it would be one problem that would lead to the quarrels, and that was money. He was working in the clothing industry, in the cutting room, and so was earning slightly more than some of his colleagues, but still we could not manage on his pay. It would be used up before pay day and there would be no money to pay for food for the babies. And the thing that made me most furious was that while we were going without small things for the home he would still manage to be such a natty dresser. That was something none of us could fathom about our men in those days, especially the uneducated ones, who would spend all their money on clothes imported from the USA. Perhaps they were trying to maintain their dignity, which they felt was stripped from them in the terrible oppression we suffered, and they needed to look smart in those imported clothes, as if to say, Look, I'm so smart, I am human after all. And I know that Roger felt very moody sometimes after work because they may have screamed and shouted at him for some mistake that anyone could have made. But the fact remained that we were poor, and we could not afford to waste any part of our money.

In 1955 we moved into our own four-roomed house in Orlando West, which is in Soweto. The arrangement was that you would pay rent, and if you could afford to pay for thirty years then you would be granted the lease of the house, but never the freehold, because the law forbids black people to own freeholds. That is the privilege of whites only.

Well, it was our pride to have such a big house. Such luxury! We even had our own yard, for a garden or vegetable plot. But the financial problems came with us. These new homes were not electrified, and this added to our difficulties, because just to have light in the evening cost us money we did not have, and the rent was always increasing.

I kept on thinking, 'It will improve.' When we had our fights I would try hard to get money together so that I could take my kids and travel to Mafeking, which was just twelve hours by train, to go to my mother-in-law, who always welcomed me.

In our tradition, when a girl married she was married, body and soul, into the family of her husband. And after the wedding, before she went to live with her husband, all the elderly women – grannies, aunties, mothers – would convene a meeting where she was told what to do when she got to her new home. All the taboos were spelt out – how to behave to her husband, her parents-in-law. And especially she was told never to expose the dirty linen in public. This is why it was always to my mother-in-law that I would go when things got really bad between Roger and me, because wife-battering was regarded as dirty linen, and a woman would suffer that in silence and never admit to a doctor what was the real cause of her injuries. Only nowadays, and this I am pleased to be able to say, this practice has been exposed to such an extent that we have refugee centres in our townships, something that was unheard of a few years ago. But then I would say to the doctors, 'I fell', or 'I tripped myself'. And his mother would be furious, and even when he'd calmed down and wanted me to come back she'd say, 'No', but she didn't mention divorce. That wasn't the language we spoke. For her, the way to get away from him was to stay with her.

But one day we started arguing and I said to my husband, 'I'm going to leave you. I'm going home.'

And this man knew I cared about my family, my family unit, and he thought I'd never leave him. So he just said, 'If you want to go, why don't you?'

I took my bag – no clothes or suitcases – and I left. I walked to the bus stop and took a bus all the way to my father's place, and that's the last time I walked away from my husband.

My children came afterwards. My people had to go and fetch them. It was not possible to do it any other way.

2

Push Your Arse!

I left my husband in 1959. In 1956, when I was twenty-six, I had started work in Johannesburg, at a clothing factory called Henochsberg's which provided uniforms for the government forces. It was my first job, apart from working as a nanny to white children when I left school, and I had not begun to develop any political awareness. But I was already angry. The hours my father had been forced to work had contributed to the break-up of my family, and my own need to earn money had put paid to my schooling. And now, when my three children were still young and I could have done with being at home to look after them, I was having to go out to work to earn a tiny wage, which we needed in order to survive.

I found the job through the Garment Workers' Union. Lucy Mvubelo, a woman I admire so much for all she did in those years for her union, was the General Secretary, and she said to me, 'Go to number one, Charles Street, they are looking for people there.' I went, and within three days they had taken me on as a trainee machinist.[1]

The factory was just opening then. I think it was about the second or third week that it had started running. I started off in a branch factory and then, after about a year, moved on into the central factory, in Commissioner Street. In the branch factory there were no white machinists. It was only when I got to the central factory that there was a mix of black and white on the shop floor.

---

[1] Sadly, in the last few years, Lucy has not been held in high esteem because of her changed political outlook. She now works for the right-wing South Africa Foundation and opposes sanctions.

I remember my first day very clearly. It was November, and when I walked into that building it seemed to me that there were hundreds of people rushing this way and that, and a terrible volume of noise, with a lot of shouting – 'Come on, do your job!' – that kind of thing. It was completely bewildering. Immediately I got there, on my first day as a worker, I was started on the machines, working very close to people who had already worked as machinists at other factories, so I was a struggler from the start. I remember most of all how they cursed us when we couldn't keep up. I was in a department headed first by an Afrikaner called Mrs Smit and then by a German-speaking man, Mr Becker. He used to shout and scream at us, sometimes for no reason at all, and it wasn't unusual for ten people to be dismissed a day. They were always saying you had to push. They would say, *'Roer jou gat',* which means, 'Push your arse' – 'Come on, push your arse and be productive'. You would be on the machine sweating, but they would tell you, *'Roer jou, roer jou'* – 'Push, push, push', and you would push and push. No one would ever say, 'Okay, that's enough. Good.' You were working for a target. You'd know there was a target you had to meet, and at the back of your mind you were concerned about the welfare of your children. You would be torn in two, because you were at work and in your mind you were at home. This is the problem of the working mother: you are divided. You are only working because you have to.

Penny was almost three when I moved to the central factory, and she'd started going to a crêche nearby, so I didn't have a baby that I had to carry from one place to another, because even though I stopped work much later than the crêche closed, and after my other two children came home from school, I had a neighbour who wasn't working, and she looked after them. But still at work you were thinking of the children, and at home you were thinking about the job, and then you had this extra person to bother about – a husband.

I'd start factory work at seven-thirty in the morning, after travelling about thirty kilometres to get there. Other workers came from double that distance. People think Soweto is the only township in South Africa, but there are many others, like Tembisa and Alexandra, and all of us would be flocking to the centre of Johannesburg for our jobs. People would be sleeping on the trains. Some would have been travelling for a long time, and even before the train there would be some distance to go for a bus stop, and the bus would already have been travelling and picking up more people. So if you had to be at your machine at seven-thirty you would have to be at your work-place by seven, and you would have to be ready to take the train at five. For some it could be about four.

I would leave my children sleeping, and the night before I would have made my preparations for the coming day, because I had to leave everything – bread, uniform, everything – lined up for my neighbour, who would come and wake my children for school. There would be nothing for you at the factory – no tea, no coffee. The tea-break was at a certain time, and if you had brought something from home that would be when you would eat, in that ten-minute tea-break later in the day. And if you had brought nothing, your tea-break would be exhausted while you were walking to the canteen and queuing there. By the time you got your coffee and sat down, five minutes had gone, and you would have to swallow everything and then run to be back on time.

I would get home about seven – and in winter, you know, that was pretty dark. When I got home I'd start making a fire on my coal stove. I used to try to prepare for that the night before, but if not I would have to start chopping wood, getting the coal, getting the ashes out and all that. And there was no one to follow my children when they were getting up, and the basin would be full of dirty water, and I would start emptying that as well, picking up the dirty clothes, and the school clothes they took off when they got home from school, and all that before I actually started cooking.

My husband would not be rushing to come home. What would he rush to come home for? When he got out from his job he would go wherever he wanted to, and because he was a man it had to be so. I couldn't question him, or ask him, and anyway when he got home my time was interfered with because I had to have water to give him to wash his hands – not just ordinary cold water, but warm water. While my fire was still burning I would pump the primus stove quickly to get the warm water for my dear husband to wash his hands, and then with the remaining water I would make tea. I would also enjoy that, but standing, because my fire would be burning for me to cook our main meal. My husband would sit and read the newspaper – and sometimes I would wonder if he really understood what he read, or if he just knew that the white boss sits when he comes home, and reads his newspaper.

I never thought to compare. I never thought that while the white boss was doing that, sitting and reading, there was a black man or woman doing everything for them. It was just the order of the day that I had to do everything. And if, after he washed, he emptied the water instead of just leaving it standing, I would be so grateful. I would feel that was so nice of him.

So then I'd cook and give them their food and everything, and if he was tired he would maybe want more water to wash his feet, because he had been standing and maybe he reckoned I'd been sitting at the machine. And then they would go to sleep, and there was the tidying up to do, and the dishes, because that was the only time I had to clean my house, at night, after everyone had gone to bed. I would do the washing as well, at night, and in the morning I would get up and before I left I would hang my washing on the line. We none of us had so many clothes that we could last the week, and so I couldn't do all the washing at the weekend. Then, on alternate days, I would do the ironing, with those heavy irons you put on the stove, and my table would be my ironing board.

My children would do their homework by candle-light. Our only other means of light was a paraffin lamp, which smelled very strong, so to me a candle was an improvement. There was never any time for me to help them – all I could do was make sure they got on with it. I could never open a book to see. My children say they cannot work for longer hours because they must oversee their children's homework. This is all foreign to me. I could never do it with my children, even though I had been educated to a good standard, because there simply was not time.

There was no time to sit and laugh and talk. No time and no energy. Even going to church, trying to cope with catching them, getting them to wash, finding their socks, always shouting. Only on the way there, walking out of that house and holding their hands – I think that was the only loving time I had with my children. Just holding their hands and walking with them to church.

That was the happiest time. They would be sitting there, and going off to Sunday School or whatever, and you could sit down and relax, and listen to someone. Even today I love to go to church, only now my company is my grandchildren instead of my children.

The church was my one pleasure, until we working women got together and had what we called *stokvels*. A *stokvel* is a neighbourhood group that is very supportive, socially and financially. Many black women earn meagre wages and cannot afford to buy the necessary comforts of a home, so we set up these *stokvels*, where we could pool our resources. You have to be a member to enjoy the benefits of a *stokvel*, and they are properly run. The members decide what is the greatest need. It could be a ceiling, a refrigerator, or pots, or anything that you could not pay for yourself. The members collect money in proportion to their wages, and put it into a pool for one person in the group to purchase what has been decided. After that they pass on to the next person, and the group identifies another pressing need, and so it goes until you find that each person in the group has managed to buy some household gadgets without getting into a hire-purchase contract, which has been disastrous to many a housewife.

Another important aspect of *stokvels* is social. Women in the townships are very lonely because their husbands tend to leave them at home when they go to soccer matches, or to the movies, or to taverns to have a drink with the boys. The *stokvel* meetings change from one member's house to another, and you are obliged to serve tea or drinks. After the money has been collected the women start conversing about current affairs, sharing their problems, which leads them to politics. And that is why African women are often much more politically aware than their Coloured and Indian counterparts, who do not have the opportunity of meeting in such a way.

That was the way my neighbourhood was. My house was the second from the corner, and there were no fences dividing the houses from each other. The woman in the first house from the corner worked in a white kindergarten, and she would be able to bring leftovers of sandwiches from rich children, and as she had no young children of her own she would pass those leftovers to me. And so we sustained each other, woman to woman – a woman-to-woman sustaining.

On Sunday afternoons, after church, I would start preparing for the coming week. It would be our first time to have a hot meal, perhaps. And there would be more cleaning. We believed in cleaning those houses. They were our pride. What else did we have to show pride in? Only our little rooms were our pride.

*

I struggled from the first day I got into the factory. After I had learned the machine better I thought that perhaps the most important thing was to do whatever I had to do perfectly, but because I wanted to do this I couldn't produce the number of garments I was supposed to. It was not possible to chase perfection along with production. They made the choice for you, and they wanted production.

As a result of my attempt to work in this way I was screamed at more than anyone else, but still I couldn't get myself to work as fast as all those other people. Every morning when I walked into that factory I really thought, 'Today it will be my turn to be dismissed.' But then I was elected a shop steward, and soon after, to my surprise (though looking back it does not seem so unexpected), I was promoted. It was after about three or four years, and I was promoted first to be a set leader and then a supervisor, which was unheard of – a black supervisor in that factory. Instead of dismissing me, they were trying to make me one of them.

We were members of the Garment Workers' Union Number 3. There were three garment workers' trade unions at that time. The Garment Workers' Union Number 1 was for whites, headed by Johanna Cornelius, and Number 2 was for Coloureds and Indians. Number 3 was for blacks, headed by Lucy Mvubelo, who had sent me to Henochsberg's in the first place. The union for Africans wasn't registered, of course, but the employers accepted it was there. Our subscriptions at that time were deducted from our pay and went to the Number 1 and 2 unions, who would negotiate for working conditions and wages for garment workers. We had an agreement which served for all three branches – whites, Indians and Coloureds, and Africans – and we would benefit from their negotiations in that whatever minimum wage was set we would be paid that amount. The other workers would get over and above that wage, but they would be sure to set a minimum wage for the African workers. In my factory we black women workers made up about 70 per cent of the work force, all earning that basic flat wage. There was no machinery to challenge that wage. It was for the employer to decide to pay over the minimum wage. It was purely voluntary, and that is in fact what it was called, a 'voluntary increase'. So our union just had to sit and wait for what came out of the negotiations with the Industrial Council. Any action we took over their decision was illegal. For us to strike was illegal.

None the less, on occasion we did strike, or go on a 'go slow'. I think the strikes that meant the most to me were in the early 1970s, when we fought to earn an extra cent, and also to narrow our hours. When I first started work the day would be from seven-thirty to four-thirty, and we fought, all of us, for the narrowing down of the time, and succeeded in bringing it down to five minutes past four for leaving the factory. We were fighting for a forty-hour week, and in the course of the fight we did go out on strike.

But even more important than the narrowing of hours was that extra cent. By then we were all earning 10 rand 50 cents a week, and only workers earning more than 10 rand 50 cents could contribute to the Unemployment Insurance Fund.

Unemployment insurance was a key issue for me, and I was very glad to have been elected a shop steward and that it was part of my duty to go about and influence people. It's strange, really, that I didn't expect to be elected, but when it came I was more than ready to accept the job. I'd say that has been true of my entire career – that I have never sought to be elected to positions of such responsibility, but when they have been offered to me I have found great fulfilment in the work they entail. You have to work hard, and learn and learn, and work even harder, because you don't have the experience, but despite this, and despite the strain, at the end of the day I can say I have enjoyed my work. Often I can't believe how any particular success or achievement has come about, and I say to myself there is no way I could have managed it, except maybe with God's grace.

On the occasion when we fought for our extra cent, I remember what a struggle we had, and how hostile the employers were. We went on a go slow strike, and they were so angry, being used to dismissing us for the least mistake, for being late or whatever. It took months for us to win – but when we did, we felt joy, great joy.

I had a dual role in the factory, but I was very clear where my first loyalty lay. I was appointed a supervisor, but I was *elected* to be a shop steward by my fellow workers.

As a supervisor I had some access to Mr Becker, who was held in very high esteem by senior management. He was very much feared by the workers, since he had a way of goading, pushing and bullying them to produce more garments than any of his white colleagues who headed other departments. He was a slave-driver. But as a shop steward I was able to intervene and reduce the numerous dismissals which were taking place.

Circumstances forced me to protect my colleagues. I pointed out to Mr Becker how counter-productive it was constantly to be dismissing people after I had trained them, and that while it was very easy for him to throw people out, it meant a heavy load of work descended on me, to start training new people all over again. Apart from the inhuman way he dismissed people, I tried to make him see that if he had constantly to train new women to be machinists or table-hands there was no way we could then achieve our work quota.

It was very unusual for a black woman to be a supervisor, and because of the superior attitudes of whites towards blacks I had to be doubly determined to demonstrate that I could do the job very well. I remember that when I first confronted Mr Becker he was quite taken aback, because he did not expect me to speak out. But with time I saw that he came to respect my views.

Henochsberg's was one of the largest factories in the clothing industry, with almost a thousand workers. We were producing uniforms for the navy, the air force, police and traffic cops. At a later stage we started production of a type of uniform totally unknown to us, which I came to realise was a camouflage uniform. These particular garments I saw on people for the first time in 1976, when on June 16 we had the uprising of the youth in Soweto, and then their massacre. At the onset of the peaceful protest there arrived in Soweto unusual types of army vehicles, from which hundreds of troops flowed out and littered the streets, all dressed in those camouflage uniforms, uniforms used for the slaughter of my people, and which I personally had helped to make. I felt horrified. There was only one non-governmental uniform we made at Henochsberg's, and that was for the Zionist Christian Church, the largest independent church, led by Bishop Lekganyane.

Evilly entwined in all the work at our factory was apartheid and all the disabilities which were imposed on us, the black workers. Job Reservation was one of those punitive decrees. Many jobs – in the cutting room, and stitching around men's jacket sleeves, for example – were reserved by statute for whites only. As a supervisor I was only permitted to supervise blacks, and forbidden by law to supervise our 'superior' whites, even though some of the jobs reserved for whites were so simple that we laughed to ourselves to see how superior they felt in performing them. The assumptions and arrogance of white South Africans never ceases to amaze and astound me, even up to this present day.

In the commercial distributive trade even the operating of lifts was reserved for whites, who were usually elderly retired people, or disabled people. Can you imagine what this means, that a tired and often retarded white person was considered more valuable and productive than a young and competent black?

In such a society as this, whites developed into very lazy people, because all the menial and hard tasks were landed on the backs of black people, and black women in particular gained from this and learned to develop resourcefulness, and talents and skills, and trained themselves to become truly competent.

Of course, we had separate facilities. Canteen, toilets, changing rooms – all these were separated according to sex and according to colour. We had to address the whites as 'sir' and 'madam', while they always called us by our first names, or, if we were being shouted at, we were called '*meid*' and '*Kaffir*'. Yet as black women, we were in the majority – perhaps 70 per cent of the workforce.

The Industrial Conciliation Act of 1956 banned the employers from deducting union subscriptions from our pay packets, so we shop stewards would have to collect all the subscriptions ourselves. We would ask to be first in the queue when we were paid, so that we could then go and stand at the gate and collect.

It was not easy to act for the workers at that time. A lot of awareness has been created over the last years, but then they were often frightened to say aloud that they were not happy with their salaries. Also, they didn't always tell their plans to me, as shop steward. They would always be surprising me. They would say to each other, without my knowledge, 'Tomorrow we are not going to start work until a certain demand is met.' I would always be early at work, because I would arrange things before the workers came in, and when I got there I would see people were not coming to start work, and I would stand there like a fool. I, a black person and a worker, would be inside with all these whites standing around with me and saying, 'Why aren't they coming in to work?' And when the whites would address the workers and say, 'What is your problem?' perhaps somebody would answer, 'We do have a problem.' So they would say, 'Who are your spokespeople? Let your spokespeople come in and talk to us.' And they would say their spokesperson was Emma, meaning me. So the whites would think I had instigated the stoppage, that I was playing a double role, making the workers stand outside and pretending I didn't know.

They could have sacked me if they had wanted. I was a shop steward, but if they wanted to sack you they could still sack you. Instead, they would try and use me to stop the trouble. They would use me like a fire extinguisher, always there to stop trouble. I would have to go to meet with the workers and ask, 'Now what is actually going on?' And they would tell me they wanted money, or they wanted that person who had been shouting and yelling at us to behave him or herself. I would listen to all that, and then I would convey it to the employers. They would be adamant, and so the workers would stay outside and not come in. Often the police would arrive with dogs and surround the workers. Many times with the help of the union we would eventually receive assistance, and perhaps the people would achieve a part of what they wanted and go back to work, But during those days, in the factory I worked in, there was one strike after another. And this has followed me all my life. Wherever I am it seems there must always be trouble.

3
Speaking Back

I don't know exactly when I became politicised. In 1955, for example, I was in Kliptown when the Freedom Charter was drawn up there, and the square that became known as Freedom Charter Square was like a stone's throw from where I was living. But at the time I really didn't know there was going to be this kind of meeting. There were many papers which were going about, and the meeting was clearly advertised, but it was only when my friends approached me that I really took notice of it.

I remember there were very many people there, and friends of mine who knew I was living in Kliptown wanted a place to sleep while they were there. This was before the African National Congress (ANC) was banned. All my friends were members, and I think the reason why I was not was because I had just got back from the rural area, and nothing meant anything to me apart from my children. It was when my friends came and spoke about this Congress that I took an interest.

The ANC had a uniform then, and these women were wearing black skirts and green blouses. The gold colour was not anywhere in them then, just green and black. So my friends were all in their colours, and I didn't have that, but every other thing which affected them and made that occasion so wonderful for them affected me as well. I was not a card-carrying member, but at that meeting I was a member in body, spirit and soul.

It was so good to be there, just to hear them speaking. Every race was there, everybody, intermingling. I would sit under the shade of a tree and listen to everything, and it was as though everything I heard was going to happen, in the next few days. I feel the same when I listen to the Freedom Charter now – just for those few moments I take heart that it will all come true, that there will be houses for everyone, schooling, prosperity, everything we need.

There were speeches against the pass laws, and cheering, and clapping, and we sang '*Mayibuye Afrika!* ' – 'Africa come back!' – and '*Nkosi Sikelel' i Afrika*' – 'God Bless Africa'. It was a moving meeting, yet with all this – the shouting, the strong talk, the mixing of races – it was a peaceful meeting. It has been a long time since we've had those kinds of meetings, with no interference or people having to run. I don't know if they'd invented tear-smokes at that time, because there was no tear-smoke, nobody running away from anything. I can't even remember seeing any police present, and the police station wasn't far from where the meeting was held. Maybe the police were there, enjoying the meeting as well, because Kliptown was the right place for this meeting to be held. It was a non-racial area. There were very many Indian people, and it was almost like a coloured area, but we were there as well. And there must have been some whites and so forth. So everyone was there. It wasn't like in Soweto, where you find only Africans, or Lenz (Lenasia), where you find Indians, or in other areas with so-called Coloureds only. It was total racial harmony.

So I think that congress was really an eye-opener for me. That, maybe, is when I started to be politicised. Although there is another thing, which I have always felt, which is that I have always resented being dominated. I resent being dominated by a man, and I resent being dominated by white people, be they man or woman. I don't know if that is being politicised. It is just trying to say, 'I am human. I exist. I am a complete person.'

The 1960s were a bad time for unions. Many were forced to go underground by the government, which was arresting people and banning meetings. The ANC and the Pan African Congress were banned in 1960, after the Sharpeville massacre, and because of the close ties of SACTU with the ANC very many union leaders had to go underground or to leave the country.

In 1962 the Garment Workers' Union, which was an all-women union, combined with the Men's Clothing Union and became the National Union of Clothing Workers, and I was elected to sit on the national executive of that union, where I stayed for twelve years. We would meet with the workers and look at their demands, and then pass these demands on to the non-African unions to negotiate for us.[1]

Soon after this, it happened that we went on strike in our factory over our wages, which were still so terribly low, and during one of our meetings somebody came from the Labour Department to drive away the representative who was addressing us at the time, one of my colleagues on the national executive. He said we had no right to go out on strike at that time, because there was an Industrial Council contract in existence, and we were therefore breaking the law. We knew nothing of this, and to us it wasn't important which law we were breaking. The important thing was that we were starving.

These meetings were an opportunity for us to speak out, and say some of the things that had been boiling up inside us, so this man – I remember he was an Afrikaner, and he had only one arm – found himself faced with perhaps more than he expected. His attitude was so rude. He didn't even introduce himself properly. The first thing he did, instead of explaining who he was and that he was supposed to be representing us, was to send our union people away, and to tell us that unions weren't recognised – meaning black unions weren't recognised – and that he was the only one who could speak for us.

Well, we challenged him, and all the workers booed him, and I, because I am not so good at booing, spoke back instead. It was very satisfying to be able to speak out and say we didn't even know who he was – that since we were seeing him for the first time we didn't see how he could be our representative, and that he was driving away the only people who had come into our factory to help us and organise us. I also asked him which law it was that we were breaking, and in what circumstances that law would not be operating, making it possible for us to go out on strike, because the Industrial Council made sure an agreement was always in operation, and that before one expired they would always have negotiated another agreement, leaving no gap in between. This was a law we had always known about. It existed already and had done since I had become a union member. But because of the suppression of the unions in those

---

[1] The national executive committee was the highest body of the GWU, elected every two years by the congress of the GWU to carry out their decisions.

years it was now being strictly enforced. And this man, instead of giving us due warning that this was the case, chose to come to our meeting and try to bully us, and drive our representatives away.

At that meeting was Tom Mashinini. He was there as an organiser, and he also was driven away by this man. We were to come across each other soon after this, when Tom was standing to be a full-time union organiser. In fact I voted for the other candidate, but I must have grown to appreciate Tom more over the next few years, since we eventually married, in 1967. He has always respected my independence, and this, I am sorry to say, is unusual in South Africa. It's also unusual to be married out of community of property, but I was. I wanted to protect Tom, because I already had my own children and he had his, and I didn't want him to be financially responsible for mine.

But all that came later. When I first saw Tom I was too angry to be very aware of him. I think it was on that day that the employers really took heed of me, because soon after I was called in to Mr Herman, the top man in the factory, who told me he had information that a strike was going to take place within a week, and that I was the one who had instigated it.

I thought he was lying, because I had no idea there was going to be any strike, and he said he'd got the information from the people in the Labour Department. They worked very closely with the police, he said, and the police had informed the Labour Department that they had been investigating the Henochsberg workers at this factory for a long time, and that I was the one who was inciting them to strike illegally. I said, 'You'll be proved wrong, because nothing of that nature is going to happen.' But unfortunately, and to my great disappointment, the workers did go out on strike that week, and Mr Herman called me in and said, 'There it is now, you see, there it is.'

Strangely, though, they still didn't dismiss me from work.

Always, when I addressed those whites, I would have to stand. We wore uniform for our work, and so I would stand there, dressed in my blue overalls, with my hands behind my back. In all the nineteen and a half years I worked at Henochsberg's I was never once asked to sit down. You just accepted that that was the order of the day when you spoke to the white boss – standing, in uniform, hands behind your back, completely deferential.

A strange thing happened with Mr Herman, though – a good thing for me, but it could have turned out badly. One day several years later, around 1970, when we were not allowed to remain in the factory during lunch-breaks, I was there filling in an application form for my daughter, Molly, who was now at the University of Turfloop. At that time I was earning around 15 rand a week, and that was after fifteen years. I used to take five rand home with me, and the other 10 rand was kept by the factory, so that I would get it all at once at the end of the year in January and be able to meet all my school fees for my children and so forth. It was very hard to live on five rand a week, but I didn't want my children ending up in the factory like I had. I didn't have much knowledge of these things. I didn't know that if I had taken the money to the bank myself there would have been some interest, which I did not get from the factory.

As I was busy filling in this form, alone in the factory, the big man, Mr Herman, walked in. I was so absorbed, putting down how I was going to pay the fees myself and so forth, and that I was separated from my husband and all the responsibility was on me, that I didn't see him. Because I am so short he could stand there and look over my shoulder to see what I was writing. I heard him say, 'What are you doing in here?' I wanted to take my papers and just run, but he said, 'No, I want to know what you are doing here.'

I apologised and told him I was filling in this form, and he said, 'You have a child at university?' I said, 'Yes.' He said, 'How do you manage to make your payment to the university?' I told him I paid it myself, out of my salary. He was so amazed, he took the form and read it, and then he said, 'Do you want me to assist you?'

Now I would say back to a question like that, 'It is the salary you give us that makes life impossible.' But then it never occurred to me. As workers, when we had our report-back from the union after negotiating, we would boo and say what we were being offered was too little, but it ended there. So when this man said it must be hard to manage with school fees and so forth, all I replied was we had to pay them. It was too fantastic that the white boss was talking to me and giving me advice, let alone saying, 'Do you want me to assist you?' We were not strong in those days, as we workers are strong today. And I was so surprised I said I would like him to give me advice, and to assist me.

I think he went home and spoke to his wife. Next day he said she wanted to meet with me, and she directed me to a group of wealthy Jewish women, the Jewish Women's Community at Temple Emmanuel. The following year an application was made for a bursary for my daughter, and I must say that then I was very grateful.

It was hard to know how to think of those whites. Mr Herman was a very polite man, a very polite white boss. He never used to shout at us. He just walked tall, with his pipe, when he came among us. We would be antagonistic to those whites on the shop floor, who were shouting and pushing us around, but this man was seen as different from them. We were deceived into thinking he was a better man. We never thought to say, 'But they are paying their allegiance to him.'

Now I think he was trying to get me where he wanted me, because when I went to meet with those women at the Temple Emmanuel he got his chauffeur to take me in his fantastic car, and when I came back the workers stood around and were amazed. To them – to us as a whole – it was the most amazing thing for me to have been in a car occupying Mr Herman's seat. I was grateful for this help, but I was aware too that I was the first to enjoy such an opportunity, and that I must not make it a secret. So I told my colleagues, and I understand that since then other workers have been referred to this organisation.

One thing that was worrying me at this time was that I could not understand why we black workers were expected to take tablets against TB, which were handed out to us as a group in our workplaces. I had heard of many bad experiences of 'medical attention', and because I felt suspicious of these tablets I protested at one of our shop steward meetings. Little did I know that the whites also were getting the same tablet, but that they received theirs person to person, and not publicly, in a group. It will always be difficult to convince us to believe that anything supposedly done for us is really to help us when it is not done for all the people as one. Among my people there are those who have learnt to be suspicious even of family planning methods, and we will always blame the side-effects that have been suffered by some of us on the fact that our treatment is of lesser importance than that of the whites.[1]

[1] One means of birth control currently given to black women and even teenagers in South Africa is Depo-provera, a long-acting progestogen. Because of the large number of sufferers from the side-effects of the drug and its banning on the North American and European markets, and because of reports by users indicating that Depo is linked specifically with weight gain, raised blood glucose levels, nausea, skin

However, after that meeting a man called Loet Douwes Dekker, a trade unionist working for the Urban Training Project (UTP),[1] approached me and said, 'Emma, I think you would be the right person to go and start a union for the textile workers.' Now all this was a foreign language to me then, and I thought he must be joking. I said no, it wasn't for me, I was okay where I was. But that wasn't the end of it. Next I was approached about a glassworkers' union, and again I didn't accept. But then I was approached by the senior people of the National Union of Distributive Workers (NUDW), the union for white shopworkers, and this time I accepted. I still don't know why, but I did. I discussed it with Lucy Mvubelo and handed in my notice.

In the suppression of the 1960s, black people had been taken out of the 'frontline' jobs in the commercial sector. Cashiering and clerical work was for whites only, and then for Indians and Coloureds as well. But now black people were again being given jobs as shop attendants and clerks. It was interesting to see this promotion of our people, but it was fourteen years since a union for black shopworkers had existed. It was to start a new union for them that I left my job at Henochsberg's on 1 August 1975.

I gave the full period of notice, but just three weeks before I left I was offered an increase of 15 rand – 15 rand, when at that time I was earning around 19 to 20 rand. They called me in and told me I'd been promoted to the position of manageress, that I would perform those duties but that on my payslip they wouldn't put my new status but would just add the extra money inside the envelope. It was bribery again, but this time I was on to them. I said the status was important, more than the money, and that I didn't want the one without the other. If a black person was to become a manager, then

pigmentation changes, painful menses, loss of interest in sex and permanent impairment of fertility, Depo-provera has been found unacceptable for white women in South Africa.

[1] The Urban Training Project (UTP) was formed in 1970 as 'an educational or service organisation' for labour organisations, and in 1978 contributed to the formation of the Black Consultative Committee of Trade Unions (BCC), which permitted dual membership of Cheif and TUCSA. The UTP also contributed towards the formation of the Council of Unions of South Africa (CUSA) in September 1980, which adopted a black exclusivist approach but retained links with the UTP and its white advisers.

everyone should know about it. It would be an important step for the black workers at Henochsberg's.

So they hid behind the Industrial Council, which was solely administered by whites, and said that because of the policy on Job Reservation they would have to refer my case there, to receive confirmation that it would be all right to acknowledge openly that I was a manageress.

There was more to come from those whites at Henochsberg's though. The day before I was to leave, to my surprise, Mr Becker called me in at about three-thirty and said, 'The Hermans would like to see you upstairs.' (There was more than one Herman at Henochsberg's – I suppose they were like a dynasty there.) When I got upstairs they were gathered there and the eldest Mr Herman told me they had agreed I was to finish that day, and then gave me an envelope. Inside was my exact pay, and not a penny more. After nineteen and a half years, that was all they gave me. And then they said, 'Goodbye'.

I was too surprised to say anything. I didn't find out until later that the workers were planning a send-off for me and that there would have been chaos – a work stoppage and so forth. The workers were very disappointed not to be able to go ahead with their plans for the next day, and as I was bidding them farewell and leaving the factory they said to me, 'We don't think, wherever you're going, that it will be very long before you're arrested for some of the things you're saying. You have taught us so much. We will miss you.'

4

Birth of a Union

Morris Kagan and Ray Altman were my first real experience of friendship between whites and blacks. I had met them before, along with other white trade unionists, at TUCSA meetings, since the NUDW was an affiliate, and I had admired the brilliant speakers there. One woman especially, Bobby Robarts, who was working for the NUDW, was a fine speaker, and she was one reason why I accepted the job – because of the challenge. But it was those two, Morris and Ray, who supported and helped me in a new way, especially Morris.

They acted as officials for both NUDW and the National Union of Commercial and Allied Workers (NUCAW), which was formed in order to represent Coloured and Indian shopworkers. I was starting the union for black shopworkers from scratch, most of the leaders for the original union having been detained or having left the country. My starting salary was 200 rand a month, which was a big jump, and to cover our first few months Kagan's union gave our union a 1000 rand loan, interest free. We were to be called CCAWUSA: the Commercial, Catering and Allied Workers' Union of South Africa.

The union offices were in Princess House, in the centre of Johannesburg. My office was on the second floor. Because of the Group Areas Act we could not, as blacks, rent offices in town, so Morris Kagan rented my office in the name of NUDW. I had an office, a desk and a chair.

My first day was a terrible experience. I had come out of a factory of over a thousand workers, with the machines roaring for the whole day, everybody busy, people shouting and so forth, and here I found myself all alone. The silence was deafening. It was spring, and I was very cold in that office. I was afraid. There were no formalities to be gone through, I just had to get myself ready to go out and find some members. I didn't know where to start or what to do. When I went home that afternoon I thought I'd made the worst mistake of my life.

I had never been a shopworker and I knew nothing of the ordinances and regulations. I was an ordinary factory worker. I would listen to Morris Kagan speaking and quoting and quoting, and I just thought, 'My God, will I ever catch up?'

In a way, this was my university education, at last, my chance to study. And I was lucky to have a man like Morris Kagan to talk to me and say, 'Here are the books. Read.'

Morris came from Latvia, and arrived in South Africa around 1929, when he was about twenty. He started working as a bus driver and bus conductor, and ended up working in a shop, and from there he became very active as a union member, eventually becoming a full-time union official. He was a junior to Ray Altman, who was a very educated man. Altman was in Cape Town, and Kagan and I were in Johannesburg.

All my admiration goes to Morris Kagan, who struggled with me. He used to say that I reminded him of his late wife, Katie Kagan, who was as short as myself and was a trade unionist ahead of him. He would say, 'Until you are as efficient in your work as the capitalists, you will never beat them.' Even the last time I saw him, the day before he died, in 1983, he scolded me because the name of CCAWUSA was not correctly spelt in the telephone directory. After that he said, 'I'm tired and I want to sleep. You will all have to go.' (I was there with Alan Fine and Morris's son-in-law.) 'First, Emma, put me properly on my pillow and cover me with my sheet. Okay. All of you – go.' And by the time I got home there was a call from his daughter to say he had died.

I invited many black unionists to his funeral. There were more blacks than whites there, and we sang '*Nkosi Sikelele*'. I thought it was important that Morris Kagan should have a funeral that would show what kind of life he had lived. I remember one elderly white union colleague asked me, 'Emma, could I have the same as Morris Kagan at my funeral?' But Morris had deserved it.

One disappointment was later on, when his family held the unveiling of his tombstone, and they didn't invite me. They knew

Morris would have wanted me there. But, well, Morris rests in peace. I honour him. People like Morris Kagan and Alan Fine were always there to offer moral and practical support.

There were other black trade unions that were being set up at that time. Every union was busy getting on its feet, and although their focus wasn't on the particular industry we were representing, at least it was on other problems that we shared, like legislation or recognition. That was very helpful and good – to work as black unions together, not just with Morris's union which was registered and recognised. Even when we worked with unions belonging to FOSATU, for example, we weren't tempted to federate with them because the FOSATU leadership was dominated by white intellectuals, and although we valued the support of its unions we did not want to be swallowed up by their way of thinking.

I needed all the support I could get, because it was clear from the start, in 1975, that the employers weren't going to make it easy for me. Like other black trade union officials, I had the problem of access to the canteens at tea-breaks and lunch-breaks, to meet with the workers at their different workplaces. The employers had just reintroduced the liaison committee system, just when we were starting our union. These committees had been formed by the government in the 1950s, to replace black unions, but they had hardly ever been used. Now they were being brought back, to water down the effects of the trade unions that were emerging, so that the workers should choose to serve in them rather than risk being union members. The committees were allowed to talk about such matters as food in the canteens, but not about the working conditions or wages. The white organisers had the advantage of going in to the stores during their breaks.

This was my first great battle. I had to spend time finding the members of the liaison committee, and where they lived, and to try and visit them. As fate would have it, most of them were men. But although in our society men looked upon women (and still do, or would like to) as the weaker sex, they did respond to my appeals, and I think the reason for that was that they respected the risk I was taking in doing this work, and that they trusted my commitment to the workers. In December we managed to achieve 200 members, and by 1977 we had reached 1000!

Our elected chairperson came over to us from one of the liaison committees, and he was a very dedicated man. His name was Johnny Rampeba, and he worked for the Checkers group, one of the biggest South African supermarket chains. He was a very valued chairperson, but he fell victim to one of the management strategies, because they realised he was a strong influence in the workplace and immediately promoted him to a managerial position. Then, when he devoted his energies to that position and gave less time to his union work, they demoted him.

The obstacles they put in our way! They were so determined not to let us near the workers. Not only did I have no access to the stores, but even distributing leaflets out in the different shopping centres brought me to my first brush with the police.

The best way of getting the leaflets distributed, to get information across to the workers about the fact that there was a union called CCAWUSA, and where the headquarters were, and what it could do for them, was to go to their workplace and wait for them to come in to work. They had their meals in the canteen, and it was difficult to catch them going home because most of the stores had several different doors, and you wouldn't know where to wait. So I would try to catch them in the morning, as they came streaming in to work.

Management was very upset by this. They used to blame me for making the workers late, even though all I did was hand them the leaflets as they went in. Then they challenged me with trespassing on private property, which was quite interesting, since if I wasn't trespassing as a shopper then I wasn't trespassing by being there with my leaflets. But then the management would phone the police, and the police would come with their dogs, often very many of them, and bundle me into their van, leaflets and all. Oh, it was disheartening to see all those leaflets disappear into their hands, with all the printing that had gone into them. And they would mishandle me, but there was nothing they could charge me with, and that was more important to me than any fear of being injured. I remember the first time they came roaring up to me with their vans and packed me off to the police station, I was horrified, thinking I was now a criminal. I had broken no law, but that was my main fear.

I was married to Tom by this time, and he would help me out, either standing with me to hand out leaflets or driving me around to the various points before dropping me at work and then going on to his own work. He would sometimes be taken to the police station along with me, but we kept on popping up the next day, at a different place, and a different set of police would come and take us away again.

What the police were not aware of was that by intimidating me in full view of the workers they were in a way assisting me, because the workers became interested in this woman who was being arrested, as it seemed, and wished to know who I was and what was going on. So I didn't give up, and when I managed to save up and buy a very old second-hand Fiat car and to learn to drive it properly I could visit many more people. It wasn't easy learning to drive at the age of forty-six, but I was glad I did!

Morris Kagan and his union were pushing very hard for the employers to meet with me. I remember a meeting with Ray Altman and his executive which I went along to. The employers were very upset about it, and asked them never to bring me again. I hadn't even opened my mouth at that meeting. I had just been there, sitting like a statue, and never uttering a word, but they were not happy about it. When Morris Kagan insisted, they said to him, 'Okay, if you want her to come along she can come, but we are not going to discuss any trade union matters with her. We are going to ask her about the weather, ask her about what is going on in Soweto. We are going to be kind enough to offer her a cup of tea and that is the most we will do.' And I said to Morris, 'I am not prepared to go and meet with anybody who wants to come and discuss the weather with me and to discuss what is going on in Soweto. My interest is in what goes on in the workplace, not in what goes on in Soweto.' But we decided then that the day would come when the employers would have to meet with me, and it did, sooner than they expected.

One morning in 1977 workers at the Checkers store in Benoni, about thirty kilometres east of Johannesburg, decided to go out on strike for an unfair dismissal that took place within their store. When they went out they didn't stay in the store but took a train from Benoni and travelled all the way to come to the union office – to me!

This was a great moment, very exciting, but I was nervous. These workers were going to lose their jobs. I had to seek advice, and I was advised to telephone their employers and tell them that the workers were out on strike and were here. I did that. I telephoned, and the employer, who was one of those who didn't want to meet with me before, said, 'Well, Mrs Mashinini, could you send the workers back to us because we have been looking all over for them.'

Well, the whole store was outside my office in the centre of Johannesburg – about fifty or sixty people – and this time I felt that the ball was in my court and I was not going to make life very simple for these employers. I said to him, 'No, I am not sending the workers to you at your headquarters. The workers chose to come to our union offices, therefore you must come down and meet with me and the workers in our offices.'

Oh, they pleaded with me – 'Please don't let the newspapers know about it' – and I said, 'Okay, if I don't let the newspapers know about it, you too equally don't let the people from the liaison committee know about it, because if they do they will come, and they will come with the police, and there will be police interference in the matter.' They promised not to, and they didn't. And when they did come into our union office they discussed the grievances of the workers in the presence of the workers, and for the first time the workers were so outspoken I didn't have much to do. I didn't have to tell them what was what. They spoke for themselves. The person who they had come out for – his name was Phineas Moriani – put his case across, and they all supported him and brought up their own grievances.

The employer simply said, 'You all go back to work. No one is going to be dismissed. You are going to be paid for the time you have been away from work.' In fact they did not go back to work that day, as it was too late. They went back the next day.

But, you know, the grievances were just unfair. For example, people would come in late because of transport facilities not being perfect, and would be given warnings. Or one would say, 'They say my uniform is dirty, but I only have one overall – how can I keep it clean for the whole week when it is the only one I have?' These small matters were made to seem very bad.

This kind of thing continued, a work stoppage here, a work stoppage there, and employers who did not want to see me before were now interested to have me come and diffuse whatever problems had occurred in the store. It is very interesting about our South African white friends, that as much as they do not want to have anything to do with you, once there is a problem they need you to come and correct the situation. I'd say to them, 'We should not be used as fire extinguishers,' because they would kindle the light and then want us to come in and put out the fire.

Even then, with their need of me, I could not be like the NUDW and NUCAW organisers, with access to the stores. Still I had to stand around on street corners and collect the subscription fees, which were one rand at that time. But even so, I was careful to keep it official. I had had my good training from my friend Morris Kagan, ~n~ I gave them receipts for every rand they paid.

The strange thing was that when I did get proper recognition for CCAWUSA from an employer, it was less of a step forward than I had expected. It happened in March 1977, and the company involved was Pick 'n' Pay.

The *Financial Mail* had been carrying articles that Pick 'n' Pay were not engaging black cashiers but were engaging black people to do other jobs. To be a cashier there you had to be a foreign worker, a white refugee, coming from Angola or Zimbabwe, or wherever. Ray Ackerman, the managing director, was challenged about this, but he just said there were no black workers available. There were, and everyone knew it. All they needed was training.

Now Ray Ackerman was beginning to feel he was being seen in an unfavourable light, and because many companies at this time were becoming concerned with their image, as a result of international pressure, he invited me to a meeting, along with Morris Kagan, and made sure everyone knew about it.

When we arrived at his offices, he delayed the start of the meeting by asking me what the relationship was between myself and Tsietsi Mashinini. I had come across Tsietsi in 1976, during the upheavals in Soweto. It was a day I remembered well, as I still do.

I was at work, and I received a phone call saying I should stop work and go to Soweto immediately. I took a taxi home, and everybody was doing the same thing, but we were stopped by road blocks and had to get out and walk. By that time we had the Black Women's Federation, and we did everything we could to protect the young students from attack. Tsietsi Mashinini was said to be the leader of the Soweto students, and since then he had become quite notorious with the authorities. He had gone into exile a few months later, to escape arrest.

I told Ray Ackerman I wanted him to know that Tsietsi's father and my husband were brothers, and that he was therefore as good as my own child. Then he said, 'Oh, well, for telling us the truth I think we accept you at this meeting.' It seemed I had to pass a test before he could accept I was an honest person.

So the meeting began. They wanted to know what our subscriptions were, how we were going to assist the workers better than they could with their liaison committee. I told him, and I told him about the Group Funeral Scheme, which cost one rand, and would pay out for a death in the family. We had much more to offer the workers than the liaison committee, and Ray Ackerman couldn't deny this.

After that meeting we were given access to the canteens at tea-breaks and lunch-times, and we had a kind of recognition with Pick 'n Pay, though no formal agreement. The policy on black cashiers changed only very slowly, but on the whole we felt we had been successful. But when it came to enjoying our success, we found that the workers became very suspicious and confused. 'Are you part of management?' and 'Why are you granted this access?' they would ask, and in the end I didn't make much use of my newly won freedom of access because the workers trusted me on the corners more than they did in the workplace.

Our first member had come from OK Bazaars, which is South Africa's largest retail company, and in 1978 I had the chance to go and speak for the workers there, who were earning less than 200 rand a month.

I had to go with NUDW representatives, but at the time I didn't care how I got there. Dulcie Hartwell, a white woman, who in 1954 was the first General Secretary of TUCSA and who became branch secretary of NUDW, was there.[1] We had a lengthy argument, with all of us pressing for a minimum wage of 200 rand a month, for a six-day week, from eight in the morning to about six in the evening, or about two on Saturdays.

They did promise to raise the wages – not up to 200 rand, but giving the lowest paid workers an increase of about 20 rand and the others 10 rand or so. Again, it was good to have a success for the workers, and to have the chance to speak for my black members, even if it was in the company of NUDW.

One thing I insisted upon, when asking NUDW to convey a

[1] Dulcie Hartwell is today General Secretary of the National Union of Distributive Workers.

message from us to management or when management, in trouble with their workers, called upon me to help them out, was that CCAWUSA was for black workers only, and when I spoke for shopworkers, I was speaking for black shopworkers. This was not simply keeping clear the distinction imposed by the South African government, between blacks, who could in theory not be union members, and other workers. Our insistence on CCAWUSA's black identity was important for other reasons too.

Our problems were very different from the problems of those white and Coloured workers; and this was vital to us as a group, to keep together in order to tackle injustice. We felt this in 1979, when the chance came to join with NUDW and NUCAW. They could not have included us before and stayed registered, but when the law changed they began to tell us they wanted to form a single union.

Decisions in trade unions are never made by the officials but by the people who are making up the union itself. Decisions come from the workers, and in this case the workers voted against forming one union. It was hard for us to forget that in the 1960s, when blacks were ousted from trade unions, the white trade unions acted very quickly in that process, and did not demonstrate for us. I could remember, for example, that the Garment Workers' Union, which I had belonged to, had been compelled to disaffiliate from TUCSA because certain unions didn't feel 'comfortable' with black unions belonging.

Morris Kagan understood this quite well. Maybe the ones closest to him did not. But in any case we remained a blacks only union until 1984, when the CCAWUSA constitution was amended to admit Coloureds and Indians, and in 1985, a few months before COSATU was formed, we removed all reference to race from our constitution.

It is hard for black workers in South Africa to identify with other workers' problems. Other workers are seen as human beings, and the black workers are seen as underdogs. And it was not exactly a common thing to see a white person speak out against their own promotion for the sake of a black fellow worker. It is all the menial jobs, all the lowest jobs in the workplaces, that are the jobs of the black workers. And as a black worker, if I speak about a transport problem I am speaking about a different transport problem from anything the white worker will have to suffer. We have these very long distances to travel, and we have the poorest possible transport facilities, and our problems concern the pass laws and schooling, and hospitals, exhaustion, and poor diet. And while white mothers have problems of their own, such as having to see one of their boys leave to fight on the border, we can understand them, because we also must lose our children – to the security forces, or to fight against apartheid. But white mothers in this country do not have to suffer anxiety over what we call breadline problems. There is no other word for them. Breadline problems are questions of who will care for the children when their mother goes to work? Who will pay the bills when the grandmother or friend cannot come one day and the mother must stay at home, even though she is not paid enough to be able to afford to lose that one day's money? Who will pay when she has to spend a day at the hospital waiting for an appointment?

No. Our problems are not the same. We had to fight for our identity as a black union. And we had to fight the dependency we had on the white workers and their unions. It was vital that we should be recognised for who we were, and that we should fight for our identity and respect as human beings. That was the battle we had to fight then. And human dignity is the battle we still must fight.

5

A Force to be Reckoned With

By 1979 it had become clear to us that the demand for the union was far greater than we could cope with, and that, as our list of postal members showed, we could no longer concentrate just on the Johannesburg city centre. We decided there was a need for a second full-time official in the union, and appointed Vivian Mtwa, who was quick to focus on workers in the West and East Rand. Then we began to make plans to establish an office in Durban, where Vivian Mtwa finally worked.

Once again we were helped by the NUDW, and by Dulcie Hartwell in particular, who was based in Durban at that time. I went there myself to talk to the workers, and I remember very clearly one incident that took place when I was organising in Pick 'n Pay, Durban North, and had stayed in the store until quite late at night.

Not being familiar with Durban, I had ordered a taxi to take me back to the city centre, where I was to meet with a friend who was putting me up. When the taxi arrived, I saw the driver looking for the person who had ordered it, and went over to him. He looked at me and said, 'Sorry, we don't take blacks in our cars.' Then he drove off, leaving me stranded. I didn't know how I was going to find my way back to the city centre, and most of the workers had left by then. I really think I would have had to stay there all night if somebody hadn't arrived in an old van with the night watchman. He was kind enough to give me a lift when I told him what had happened.

Apart from this unpleasant incident, though, that was a good trip. The office in Durban was followed by another new office, in Cape Town, in 1980, and there we were helped by Oscar Mpetha, of the

Food and Canning Workers' Union,[1] who on behalf of his union made available enough money for us to employ another organiser and hire offices for six months.

This was, all in all, a very exciting time for black workers, because as well as the success of CCAWUSA in building its membership, the other black trade unions were also growing in size and influence. Despite the efforts of the government and employers, we had international trade links and were affiliated to international trade secretariats, so we had a very strong profile in world trade affairs. There was a lot of travelling involved, and as well as receiving support from organisations abroad we were able to provide information about South African multinationals which had companies in other parts of southern Africa, like Zimbabwe, Botswana and Lesotho, and which were paying even lower wages to their workers in these countries. As a result of this, the International Federation of Commercial, Clerical, Professional and Technical Employees (FIET) were able to put together a survey on the distributive trade in southern Africa, which was published in 1982.

In 1977, when the Wiehahn Commission was set up to look into the situation with regard to democratic trade unions, it was especially concerned to plan a strategy for dealing with black trade unions, which they saw as 'subject neither to the protective and stabilising elements of the system nor to its essential discipline and control' (Wiehahn Commission of Inquiry, report of May 1979). The government knew we were there by then, and that they couldn't push us into the sea.

When the Commission began asking people to go and make representations to them, I was elected to represent the workers of the group of unions with which CCAWUSA was working. There were several people sitting on the Commission – about twenty – but only one black man, and not a single woman, black or white. Of course, the black trade union movement was not represented. I was questioned about political involvement in the trade unions, and I didn't pretend there wasn't any. I insisted that the trade unions have

---

[1] Oscar Mpetha was arrested after the 1980 students' uprising in Cape Town and tried in the Cape Town Supreme Court on charges of murder and terrorism. He is at the time of writing serving a five-year sentence. He is nearly eighty, suffers from diabetes, and has had to have a leg amputated because of a gangrene infection.

got to be very much involved in politics, and that even if trade unions anywhere else in the world are not involved politically, in South Africa they must be, because this is a country where everything around us is politics. As they say, touch a black person and it's politics. So we cannot simply say we want to fight for our rights as workers, because politically we are not even recognised as workers. The Industrial Conciliation Act excluded us from its machinery because we weren't regarded as workers.

Well, we had our hopes of the Commission, and when the law was changed and we were informed that we could apply for registration we went ahead and did so. But I must tell you, this was not by any means an easy decision. The issue was sensitive for all the black trade unions, and there were many who felt that to register was to sign up as a willing partner in the whole unjust system of apartheid. We had a sore debate about this in CCAWUSA, and for a long time we could not decide one way or the other whether this would be the right or the wrong thing to do. In the end we did apply. We put our faith in the new law, and as a result the world was told that black trade unions were now an established part of South African society, and the government could put on a good face.

We applied for registration that year, in 1979, but we had to wait until 25 November 1981 for it to be granted. By that time I was in detention, safely out of the way. The sequence of events was this: after the law was passed, those trade unions with 'difficult' leaders were told their registration was under consideration, and then there was a swoop and those leaders were arrested. The unions were given the right to exist. But the union leaders, who had negotiated this right, were betrayed.

And in the end, registration was not as important to us as being formally recognised as the workers' representatives. We came to realise that while you can be a registered union with no members, you can force the employers to negotiate with you if you are recognised as being the union representing the workers, registered or not. We had been talking to all these companies without any recognition agreement – even Pick 'n' Pay, though they recognised us informally, had not drawn up an agreement with us – and they listened to us because they knew their workers would not accept anyone else. But now we decided it was time to get management to give us something in writing, and in 1980 we negotiated our first agreement, with Allied Publishing.[1]

The Allied workers – over 2000 of them – were very much exploited. The lowest paid, the drivers and the street-sellers, were earning around 22 rand a week for a seven-day week. They were working very long hours, starting early in the morning, about five, and not finishing until about seven, except on Sundays when they stopped at midday.

The Allied workers began organising themselves into CCAWUSA in about 1978. The shop stewards would regularly come to the union office to plan strategy and then go off organising. Little did the management know at the time that organising was made easy because the drivers who delivered the papers to depots and selling points would at the same time do the organising. This was something we had learned with our membership among the big stores. The drivers were very committed to the union, and as they delivered merchandise to the stores they would also deliver union leaflets and membership application forms.

So by early 1980, with members all over the Transvaal and Orange Free State, the Allied workers were organised well enough for the union to approach the management to negotiate a recognition agreement. We wrote asking for a meeting to discuss the workers' grievances, and they replied by asking whether we were registered or intending to register under the government's new labour dispensation. We saw this as a refusal to meet with us, and released their letter to the press, and as a result were offered an 'informal' meeting to discuss 'ground rules for a future relationship'. And Allied's acting managing director was kind enough to describe me as 'a very competent person'!

The result of these talks was an increase in wages which, although it was not as much as we were asking for, did bring them up to what we agreed was a compromise starting point for future negotiations. And by October of that year we had signed our first agreement. It was

[1] Allied Publishing distributes most of South Africa's English-language newspapers and is now owned by the Argus group, the largest English-language newspaper publishing house. Before 1983 it was jointly owned by Argus and Times Media Ltd (then South African Associated Newspapers), the other main English-language publishing group.

not a very impressive document by today's standards, but at the time we were pleased with it. It did not take even a month to show it was not good enough.

Early in November an employer assaulted a member of the union at one of their complexes, somewhere in Rosebank, and the workers decided to say, 'Gone are the days when employers can just be free to assault workers. We are not slaves. We are workers.'

It was very interesting to watch these workers flex their muscles. The newspaper complexes are scattered all over the Transvaal, but they went to one central point, the *Star* Offices, in Sauer Street, Johannesburg, to say that not a single van would leave the place until the manager who had assaulted one of their members had been dismissed. There was a standstill – no papers going to Pretoria, or the Free State, or anywhere. The management got university students to come in and do the work, but they were not as efficient, and anyway they could only deliver papers to the small retail outlets for sale. There was no one to sell the papers on the streets or to deliver them by bike to people's homes. All this time we were having meetings, and in our meetings the employers said they would take this man who was assaulted – his name was Shakespeare – to the doctor for treatment.

He wasn't badly hurt, it was just that he had been assaulted. So when we said their offer was not sufficient, it was because we had demanded that the manager involved should be sacked. This was the principle we were fighting for – that management did not have the right to physically abuse its workers. But with their attitude – the attitude that would stand affronted and say, 'We are not going to take heed of what this black union wants' – the dispute continued for days and days, and in the end they said we had violated the regulations and would therefore lose the agreement we had signed. We said with pride that we were prepared to lose the agreement, but we still demanded the dismissal of this man. Then they said they were not prepared to do this, and threatened to dismiss all the workers. With the high numbers of unemployed they could do this and find replacements, even for such a large workforce. So in the end we went back, accepting their promise to investigate the assault.

Two weeks after the strike, the manager concerned resigned, and this represented real victory to the union. To the best of my knowledge there never was another assault of that kind, and we continued to negotiate with them for better wages. And within a few months we had also negotiated a new and better agreement.

Another step forward for CCAWUSA in 1980 began with an incident in the Western Cape, when workers at an abattoir were unfairly dismissed. Because of this, and because the management had all along been very determined not to respond to the demands of the workers, there was a joint effort to support that union, the Western Province General Workers' Union (WPGWU), with a red meat boycott. The boycott spread over the whole of the Western Cape, and it had very good support. My baby sister who lives in Guguletu is married to a man who owns a butcher's shop, and they were totally out of business because red meat was not being sold and they were having to sell the chickens.

Our interest in the red meat boycott was that the employers in the strike were advised by members of the Greatermans industrial relations division, in particular by a man called Andrew Levy, who was operating an industrial relations consultancy on the side. Now Greatermans were at that time the owners of the Checkers group, who used us when things were a problem but who had still not granted us access or recognised us as representing their workers. So we took the greatest interest in this, and we decided to write a letter to the *Rand Daily Mail*, a liberal paper which has now, sadly, closed down, condemning their role in this strike and pointing out it was not surprising they had helped the employers defeat the WPGWU since Greatermans also refused to grant us recognition.

Before publishing our letter, the *Rand Daily Mail* phoned Greatermans to verify the contents, and when Greatermans heard what was going to happen they sent Levy and his colleagues to pay us a visit. I remember the surprise I had when these powerful people swept into my office, without an appointment, demanding to know how I had come to write 'such a letter', which they said was unfair. I was unable to see them immediately, because a few minutes earlier some of the senior management of Woolworth's South Africa, Eloff Street, had stormed in, also without an appointment, to protest that their CCAWUSA workers were threatening to strike.[1] So

---

[1] Woolworth's SA has no connection with the Woolworth's stores in Britain. It does have close links with the Marks & Spencer group and sells many of its products. It is the high-class supermarket and clothing chain in South Africa.

Morris Kagan and Alan Fine sat with the Greaterman people while I dealt with the Woolworth's problem first.

When I was finished I went to tell Levy and his colleagues that the reason I had been forced to go to the newspapers was that over the years the Checkers management had steadfastly refused to recognise us as representing their workers. Levy claimed that, whatever might be the case with Greatermans, he had not advised the abbattoir employers to take such a hard line. Then we got on to asking why his company was so hostile towards CCAWUSA, and in the end they agreed that since so many of their workers were members they would deduct union subscriptions from their pay, so long as the workers authorised them to do so. And this was the start of our getting recognition at the Greatermans stores.

I say the start, because it is astonishing how long such agreements can take to be put in operation. For example, I remember that when we were given access to the canteens, and were distributing our leaflets, Greatermans took exception to the wording, saying they didn't think it was in 'good taste', and we had to have a long tug of war about that. But in the end all was well and good with that company, and at the end of that day I thought back to Morris's prediction that one day those whites who refused to deal with me would come running.

Boycotts like the red meat boycott were a sign of the strength the unions were beginning to build at that time. Another sign of that strength, though not one we appreciated, was the number of leaders being held in detention. During the boycott, four union organisers were arrested under the General Laws Amendment Act, and two were held under Section 22, a provision of what was then the Terrorism Act, which permitted police to hold people for fourteen days without charge.[1] Looking back, I can see that my time was coming, and that I would not for much longer be allowed to stay out in the streets fighting for our members; then I had too much on my mind to be aware of anything apart from the job I was doing, which was shortly to involve us in threatening a boycott of our own.

This was still in 1980, and it came about as a result of a dispute involving the Black Municipal Workers' Union, which ended in the

---

[1] In 1982 the Terrorism Act was combined with a number of other pieces of security legislation to become the Internal Security Act.

biggest strike by black workers anyone could remember. They were fighting for the Johannesburg city management to recognise them, and the management was insisting on recognising a parallel 'sweetheart' union. So about 12,000 workers downed tools, and in a few days those so clean streets of South Africa were filthy and the city services were grinding to a halt.

Once again, the strike ended in defeat for the workers, and after about a week they were all sacked, forced on to buses by armed police, and sent back to the homelands. But because the municipal workers were on strike the big chain-store employers wanted the general store workers to sweep the pavements around their stores. All the big chain stores wanted this – OK Bazaars, Greatermans and Woolworth's South Africa, among others.

We had no intention of interfering with the municipal workers' strike, and we came together as a union. We put together a leaflet which we distributed to all the different chain stores, saying that none of our members should be seen sweeping around the surroundings of their stores. Woolworth's was adamant. They said they were concerned that their customers should not slip and fall from whatever mess might be around their doors. But we felt very strongly about this and we said, 'We will call a boycott if this continues.' I went into one of the stores and asked to speak to the manager, to insist that we would carry out our threat if I saw anyone sweeping the pavement. They tried to be adamant again, and I had to call the regional manager, who understood we meant what we were saying and put put out an order that no one should be made to sweep the streets.

All this in 1980. It was a good year. The power of the unions was now coming on and for the first time we were saying to employers: This or that must not happen; this must not happen to members of our union.

6

The Arrest of a Commie

All our offices were leased under NUDW, because under the Group Areas Act blacks were prohibited from leasing offices in white areas and establishments. In 1981, in order to be rid of us, the owners of the York House building in Johannesburg informed NUDW that when their lease expired it would not be renewed. The office was very modest, with a small room and an anteroom, but they clearly wanted us out.

This brought a very big change in our lives, because as head of CCAWUSA I had to go and approach Desmond Tutu, the General Secretary of the South African Council of Churches (SACC), to grant us accommodation, since no one else was prepared to have us. So we became the first union to be granted accommodation in Khotso House (House of Peace), and I found it quite amusing that NUDW, who came in also, did so under our auspices.

In Khotso House we now had access to infinitely superior accommodation. Apart from our office we had a large hall, which could hold most of the strikers from CCAWUSA, and later from other trade unions, and which was used continuously until Khotso House was destroyed by a bomb in 1988.

With the tremendous growth of union workers, education was top of our list in organising members into the unions. We therefore had to be wait-listed for accommodation at the training centres, which were mainly Catholic and Anglican Church centres catering also for other organisations. We were concerned about the amount of time and money we spent travelling to some of these centres. At that particular time most union headquarters were situated in the

Johannesburg area, because our membership was much bigger there. So we had in mind to set up a centre which could be used over weekends for training and during the week could be converted into a day-care centre or be used by the community any way they wanted.

In the end we established a committee of representatives of the progressive unions, including the African Food and Canning Workers' Union, whose regional secretary, Neil Aggett, took a very active interest in the project to build a centre. I chaired the meetings, and the secretary was Alan Fine, who was engaged by NUDW as an organiser, and who also took a very active interest in our plans. He was arrested in September 1981, under Section 22, and Neil took his place as secretary. It was a meeting of all these trade unions that year which saw the birth of an ideal which finally germinated with COSATU, and later COSATU House, which was bombed in May 1987.[1]

We thought and hoped that Alan would be released after fourteen days, and I can remember keeping some chocolate for him in a drawer as a surprise for when he came back, because I knew he loved chocolate, and I was even planning to tease him a little, by marking the calendar and telling him how much time he had wasted while we were working so hard, and that there was much work to be done and he had better get on and do it, after sitting idle for two weeks.

But then the fourteen days were up, and he wasn't released. I became very concerned for him, and it was at this time that I grew close to Neil, who would come in every day and talk with me about what was happening.

Alan was now being held under Section 6, which allowed for people to be held indefinitely. I think he was one of the first to be held under that section. There was another white trade unionist arrested at that time, Barbara Hogan, who was also a friend of mine and who is still serving a 10-year sentence, charged in 1982 with 'furthering the aims of a banned organisation', the ANC. And shortly

[1] The Congress of South African Trade Unions (COSATU) was formed in 1985 as a federation of trade unions working with the following principles in mind: (1) control for the workers; (2) non-racialism; (3) one non-racial union per industry; (4) representation based on paid-up membership; (5) national cooperation between unions. In 1988, under Order 335 of the regulations made under the Public Safety Act (1953), the Congress was effectively banned from any activities taking place outside the workplace and not directly affecting the workers as workers.

afterwards, Neil himself, another white person involved with black trade unions, was arrested, on the same day as I was.

Neil was a medical doctor who was particularly concerned with occupational therapy, and he used to come and speak to us at health and safety meetings. That was his concern with the Food and Canning Workers' Union as well. His girlfriend, Liz Floyd, was another doctor, and she had a friend called Liz Thompson, who also took a keen interest in the workers and their health. We called them Liz and Liz, and all of us used to discuss together what was happening to Alan and Barbara, but I must say we didn't connect what had happened to them with our ideas for a trade union centre. We thought instead that it must be something to do with the Wilson-Rowntree boycott, which started around this time.[1]

So I was completely unprepared when, on the morning of 27 November 1981, I woke, very early, to hear loud bangs and knocks at the door of our house. My husband opened the curtains to look out, and saw a string of cars of police and soldiers. He opened up to let them in and they swarmed into our bedroom to find me still in my night clothes. My husband and children were all ordered out of the house, just in their nighties and pyjamas, and locked out there for more than an hour.

They said to me, 'Emma Mashinini, we are detaining you under Section 22,' and that I still take exception to, because they should have made that statement in the presence of my family and not to me alone.

They searched the house, the dustbin, outside in the yard. They took complete charge of everything while I stayed in my nightie. With the shock and everything I wanted to go to the toilet, and whenever I went there was one policewoman who came with me, accompanied me literally into the toilet – as though something would come out of that place to attack them and she had to be there all the time. And they went on searching. They searched through the piles of letters from my children, and from the friends I had made all

[1] The East London branch of the South African subsidiary of the Rowntree Mackintosh confectionery group sacked 470 workers belonging to the SAAWU early in 1981, and this marked the start of a boycott of the company's products by anti-apartheid campaigners in South Africa and in York, England, which was to continue for over a year. The boycott failed to win any gains, and the sacked workers were not reinstated.

over the world, and from the shopworkers' unions in different countries.

The letters were very interesting to them, and the books, especially all the books that had something to do with trade union work. They took piles of them, piles and piles of things, and put them on the table, and just at the time when they were about to leave the house my family was called in and they said to my husband that he should attach his signature to a form saying they were taking these books and materials that had been found in the house.

Tom refused to sign. 'I am not going to attach my signature to this when I don't know whether you brought these things along with you or what.' They were very rude to him and said he was not making life easier for me, but he said he would not do it.

They did not want us to speak to one another. I said 'Tom' and was going to say that no, they did take the books from the house, but they would not let me say anything further, so it was to my advantage that they did not let us speak. At one stage they brought a black policeman who thought maybe my husband did not understand what they were saying, and he said, 'I hear each and every word that you are saying. I am just not prepared to do it.'

They took me out to their cars. Now I was in the street, and my neighbours were standing on the corners to see what was happening. It was as though they had come to arrest a murderer, a criminal. It was only about six-thirty in the morning, and I was busy working over in my mind why it was they had come to arrest me, what offence I had committed. And after some time it came to me – oh no, maybe it is like the other trade unionists who were arrested in September. And then I thought, Section 22 is fourteen days. I was counting – oh my God, fourteen days, two weeks' time, in two weeks' time it'll be . . . I'll be back, I'll be out, just before Christmas, I'll be back home . . . But why, why?

They drove me to town, to Khotso House, where we now had our offices.[1] They didn't even ask me where our union offices were.

---

[1] Khotso House is well known for housing anti-apartheid organisations. As well as the United Democratic Front, the Detainees' Parents Support Committee and the Black Sash, many church groups have offices there. Police raids like this one are a regular occurrence.

They went straight to that place to search it. And it was dead silent, dead silent in the back of the car, with me in the centre and two policemen escorting me.

Several cars had gone, but still there were about three or four that came with us to Khotso House. When we got there it was too early in the morning for the door to be open, and we were not able to open it ourselves. The policeman who was standing there said the key was not there. And the man inside would not open. He knew it was too early for there to be anybody in the offices, so anything could have happened. He was very brave and very sensible not to open, and we had to wait until someone from inside came out.

When eventually we did go in, they searched our offices, through all the files – and there was a lot of paper then, not like when I first started the union, when I didn't have one letter. Again they were interested in all of it, and again they took piles of the files and books.

It was now after eight, and the people coming to work were having to wait outside. I was still just standing around, wondering what would happen next. I did at least have a dress on over my nightie.

Finally we went out to the car again, and when the lift stopped at the ground floor we met a group of inmates of Khotso House who were coming from the chapel, because in Khotso House every morning they have prayer meetings held at eight-thirty before people start work. It had been announced that I had been seen accompanied by police and that my offices were being ransacked. Several young men came to say, 'What are you doing to Emma?' And even though the police said, 'Get away, get away,' they still came, just to show that they were with me. And when I walked out of the lift with the police carrying all the books and was taken to the cars, the people did not go into the lift, but instead they followed us. They were singing and chanting, '*Siphe Amandla Nkosi Okunge Sabi*' – 'God Give Us Courage' – about fifty of them, black and white, singing 'Give her strength, Lord, not to be scared. Give her strength, Lord, for her to stand up and face whatever they are going to expose her to.'

I was strengthened by these people, and all the goodbyes, the waving at me, and the good things they were saying, that there will come a day when all this will be over, one day. Right in front of the car they were standing, and they sang the national anthem and chanted, '*Amandla Ngawethu*' – 'The power is ours' – and I was raising my clenched fist back.

We went to John Vorster Square,[1] where I was put into a room, and there I was interrogated and harassed and given a number. And after some time I was called in by other policemen, who were looking through all the books and things which had been collected from my home.

'You're fat, Kaffir meid,' one said to me. 'You're a nuisance and a troublemaker.' And afterwards he said to me, in Afrikaans, 'Are you a commie?'

Well, my understanding of that was, 'Are you a communicant?' because I saw some Bibles and I thought he meant was I communicant of the Church. So I said yes.

And he said, 'Well, I'm not going to give you the damned Bible, because you are a Communist and you admit it.'

I was shocked, and all by myself, and it seemed everyone had an insult for me, that everyone who walked past had a word of insult to say to me. I was just in the centre of a mess. Who was I to argue over anything and say I misunderstood and that the last thing I was was a commie? That is how they work. They put you in a room, and confine you there so that you must just think you are the only person who is arrested and detained. They don't want you to be exposed to the knowledge that there are other people who are detained as well.

As fate would have it, with all the shock, I kept needing to go to the toilet, and time and time again I had to say to this lady, 'Now I want to go to the toilet.'

But this time when I went, just before we turned into the toilet, we passed the lift, and it stopped, and someone walked out and said, 'Hello, Emma.' It was Neil Aggett. I wanted to respond, to say hello back to him, but the relief of finding I was not the only one who was arrested took it away from me, and I could not bring out even that one word. I always regretted that, that I did not say hello to Neil, because I was not to see him again. But he was being pushed one way, and I that way, and he did manage to say, 'Hello, Emma.'

---

[1] The building called John Vorster Square is used as a form of clearing house. It is the last place a detained person is known to have been taken. Thereafter, every attempt is made to keep the whereabouts of detainees completely secret, in order to prevent demonstrations and any proper investigation of their conditions.

From the toilet I went back to the office where they were writing down my details. They took photographs and fingerprinted me, and later on I was taken downstairs to the car, with just the little bit of clothing I had brought with me. They told me, in Afrikaans, that they were going to drive me to the Wilds, which is a place where all the muggers and criminals hang out. One understands Afrikaans, but only as much as one has to. There is not the willingness to learn to communicate very well.

As they were driving me I was busy looking at their clock, because the radio was on and it was just about one o'clock, and I was anxious to hear the news in case there was an announcement about what was happening to me. But these people are not great fools. Just when the radio said 'pip pip pip' for the news they switched off the radio, which was my lifeline. Yes, these were young bully boys.

My mind was concentrating on that journey, and inside I had a picture of my husband, and a picture of my neighbourhood, and I was thinking that in fourteen days I'd be back.

I don't know where we went. They took me many different ways, just to cause me more confusion, and they were insulting me all the time.

But then we stopped, and I saw we were in Pretoria.

I think it was then I realised I was really in trouble. I was taken to the offices and put into a cell. And I thought then, now I am arrested. Now I am detained.

Because, to me, Pretoria Central Prison was a place for people who have been sentenced to death.

II

SP CLAMPDOWN –
NATIONWIDE MOVE

More than a dozen leading trade unionists, students and labour experts were detained early today in a nationwide Security Police swoop.

They were detained in terms of Section 22 of the General Laws Amendment Act which provides for a two-week period of detention without the detainee being brought to court.

Those known to have been detained are:

Mrs Emma Mashinini, General Secretary of the Commercial, Catering and Allied Workers' Union . . .

Security police around the country have confirmed a number of the detentions.

Reports of further detentions have not been confirmed at this stage . . .

The Star,
27 November 1981

Dear Tom,

Both Emma and you have devoted your life to the union movement, and the detention of Emma is a destructive act in that it denies her continued dedication to the workers' cause.

Attached are copies of the letters sent by UTP in regard to Emma's detention and that of the others. It is UTP's assessment that employers in particular have to account for themselves.

We will keep you informed.

Yours sincerely,

L. Douwes Dekker
Chairman

Urban Training Project
3 December 1981

To all affiliated organisations
To all members and alternates of the Executive Committee
Concerns: Arrests in South Africa

Dear Sisters and Brothers,

On 27 November a wave of arrests in South Africa of leaders in trade union, church, community and other organisations occurred. The majority are being held under Section 22 of the General Laws Act, under which individuals may be detained for up to two weeks without trial.

At the time of writing (30 November), five trade unionists are known to have been arrested, including Mrs Emma Mashinini, General Secretary of the IUF-affiliated Hotel, Liquor and Catering Trade Employees' Union HOTELICA.

In view of this situation, you are urgently requested to make representations to the South African authorities protesting the arrests and mentioning in particular that of Mrs Mashinini, and demanding the immediate release of the arrested. Representations should be made to:

Hon. P. W. Botha
Prime Minister
Pretoria
South Africa

with copies to the South African diplomatic representation in your country. In the past, the South African authorities have shown themselves sensitive to interventions from IUF unions (as well as the trade union movement in general), especially on the level of the diplomatic representation in the countries of the unions concerned. It is therefore suggested, where possible, to directly contact the representation in your country. As always, the IUF would appreciate receiving copies of all communications.

Thanking you in advance for your cooperation, I am
Yours fraternally
Dan Gallin
General Secretary

International Union of
Food and Allied Workers'
Associations
Geneva, 30 November 1981

7

Pretoria Central Prison

The cell was a very small cell. There was a toilet, there was a basin to wash. The toilet was a proper flush toilet, very clean. Extremely clean. There was a bed, and there were sheets on the bed. The window was right next to the door. It was a very small window. Through it somebody in the corridor could see you, but they had put Elastoplast on the other side so you could not see out.

I was cold. Everything was taken. I had a gold chain which my daughters had given me for my fiftieth birthday. That was taken. Everything was removed, up to my rings. I sat in that place with nothing to read. Just with myself. The bare me.

It was a prison where there seemed to be whites only. A prison of black people would not have been so clean. They would not have bothered. It was November, mid-summer in Pretoria, but I was very, very cold.

I had no visits, no interrogation, no word from anybody whatsoever. All I had was people talking behind shut doors. The white prisoners who were there were the ones who would bring the food. They were criminals and they were not allowed to open the door. They put the plate just on the doorstep until the policewoman decided to come, open the door, and push the food in. At times, when the plate had been there for some time, you could hear them talk amongst themselves. 'You know, that plate has been there for some time. It is now cold.'

I was able to count the days by my meals and by dark and light, by how many nights, how many getting ups. I was able to count that day onwards to day fourteen.

And it was still Emma. I was still sane. I was myself.

It was my solace to hear a woman talking. And then on Sundays I could hear people singing hymns. I'm sure there was a black prison not far away from where I was. I could hear their singing, and there was a song which I learnt from them. '*Simswabisile Usatan*' – 'We have disappointed the devil because he has no power over us here. We are together and the devil will never catch us again.' Thereafter I would wait for Sundays to hear these black people sing.

Next to my cell there was a lift, and on the other side of my cell was a laundry. The machines were loud and running all the time.

The food was very bad. One day I saw on my plate beetroot peel. Just that. They cooked beetroot and they took the peel and that's what I had on my plate. I started becoming hypertensive and I told them, 'I'm not going to take food with salt,' and they said, 'Well, you will have to.' And I ate. I was looking forward to going home – I said to myself, I need to eat, to keep strong to go home.

On my fourteenth day, when the policewoman came to open the door for me and brought my food in, she said would I like to go and have a bath. I thought that this meant I was going home.

After my bath, when she was locking me in, I said to her, 'Am I not going home?' She said to me, 'Didn't you see the newspapers – that you are charged with another section?' – as though I could get a newspaper. Yet I think she was not doing this to spite me but was unaware of the system, of her own system.

Now I think that was the most heartbreak I had. The heartache was even greater than when I was actually removed from home, because I was now being held under Section 6. I kept telling myself, Section 6 is one of the worst sections. You can remain in prison for an indefinite time. It depends on the government.

When the policewoman told me that she'd read from the newspapers that I was being transferred from Section 22 to Section 6, I really felt this was very bad for me, because I had known people who were there for a very long time. And now this hope of saying I would be out of prison within two weeks had gone; it was like being detained for the first time. Section 6 meant complete isolation and solitary confinement, which was no better than Section 22. Even with Section 22 I never had any visitor within those two weeks. I never had anybody to communicate with.

When I went to bed that day – well, from that day onward – I never even thought it was necessary to eat and keep strong to go home because I knew – my God, I knew – that now I'd had my chips.

They couldn't make me eat. I just did not feel hungry. So they sent in the nurse to come and ask why I could not take the food. It was a white nurse, and I told her that I could not eat the food because it was so bad. I cannot even describe it. Their bitter coffee and bread was almost better than whatever we were being given to eat.

What was more horrible was that I had to enquire from a very junior policewoman, 'Why am I not going home?' And this made me really feel something was wrong. What if I had not enquired? They may have just forgotten me when I was supposed to have gone home, and nobody would have come to tell me. I did not understand the law myself, but I really felt that there was something wrong in that I was not told. Then, you know, I really had to search myself: What did I do? What offence have I committed? In fact, no one ever told me that.

All my trade union experience of demanding to see and not being refused just fell aside. Even going to bed was an effort. I was just a lump. And this was now heading for Christmas, the time I'd always thought I'd be home. I thought about my children. My children who were not here. My one baby was in New York, my other one was in Germany. I thought, Oh my God, it will be just too much for them, to find out. If the officer read it from a newspaper it means they will get the papers and they'll know that I've been charged with a much more severe section and made to remain in prison.

With the cold still, and the horrible food, and the headaches and dizziness from the hypertension, and now this heartbreak and disappointment, this was a bad time. A very bad time.

After about three and a half weeks I was told that an inspector would be coming to visit me. I wanted to know what this inspector was for, and they said it was an inspector for Section 6 detainees.

I was taken out of my cell – my first real time out of that cell – and into an office where this inspector was, together with a black man. Whether he was a policeman or an interpreter himself I don't know. And this inspector said to me he wanted to know if there was anything I needed.

For a very long time I had had extremely cold feet, and I was tempted to tell these people I wanted to buy Vaseline and short men's socks, just to keep my feet warm, because my feet were freezing all the time. I could have told them to buy them for me because I had had five rand on the day they took me from home and this five rand was taken by the police in Johannesburg. But I thought, after all that, here is somebody who comes in as though he is a friend to ask me what I really need, and he says he will provide me with whatever I want. He said books, toothpaste and so forth. And all I said was that I didn't want anything. I mean, they can take you, isolate you, kick you, and then all of a sudden they find you a friend, as they now seemed to have. But I never made a request. He would come, I think, about fortnightly, this man, but all the time I said, 'There is nothing I want.' And when he said, 'Any complaints?' I never made any complaint. It would not serve any purpose.

They knew. They had their little window and the nurse was coming in because of my hypertension. So they knew all was not well with me. They did not need to ask what was wrong.

It was a very frightful thing, that window. Whilst I was sitting on my only sitting place – there was no chair, I had to use the bed to sit, to sleep, to do everything – I was always sitting opposite that window, which was sealed. But then when I was on the bed, trying to sleep, not expecting anybody, I would just see two eyes piercing at me. All I could see was their eyes. It was very, very frightful. I couldn't get used to it. I thought, it's like an animal, to see those two eyes, and I'm in a cage. It was frightening.

One day, two policemen came, together with a policewoman, and they said, 'Come on, come, come out of the cell.' Nothing like, 'Get yourself ready to go' or whatever. It was just 'Out' and out I went.

There was this very long corridor that I had to walk through. And along this corridor were women on their knees, and these women were all wearing the same colour of clothing. I take it it was uniform. And just as they heard the feet of the people coming, all these women went with their faces to the floor. They had to bury their faces on the ground. And we were walking, walking, and to me this is Pretoria Central Prison, where people are executed or sentenced, hanged or whatever. I am isolated, and now I am just taken from my cell and being made to walk through this very long corridor and people are burying their faces on the ground. Nobody looks up, and people are pushing me from behind – '*Gaan, gaan, gaan!*'

I'm a short person. I could not walk as fast as they did, and I had no business to. I did not know where I was going. Eventually, when we reached a doorway, they pushed a door, and there were policemen waiting, with their guns. I did not know whether I was going to be shot or what. Nobody ever says anything. These people have fine ways of torturing you. They let you torture yourself.

We went through and out into a car. Still they didn't tell me where I was going to. I didn't ask. I had no saliva. I was so thirsty – very, very thirsty. I think that was the shock. This is how thirsty I was. I saw one of those police people, it was a woman, a white policewoman, chewing gum. They were busy eating. I put out my hand to say, 'Please, I'm dying,' you know, of thirst, and she made a joke out of this. 'She wants to chew because we are chewing.' She made a joke and she never gave it to me. All I wanted was water, water, water, and I could not get water.

We drove, I think, into the centre of town, and the car was parked. Just when we were about to leave the car that white policewoman said, 'Bring your hands,' and when I brought out my hands she said, 'Let's put bangles on you,' and they put handcuffs on me.

This was my first time of being handcuffed. I wasn't handcuffed the time when I left home. And I just asked, 'Has any woman been handcuffed before?' I had never seen a woman walking in the streets with handcuffs on.

They deliberately had parked the car very far from where they were taking me. I still did not know where that was. But what a funny, strange feeling. Walking in the street, escorted by them, with the handcuffs.

I did not slump my hands, or whatever. I really held them up. I thought, I must be seen, that I'm handcuffed. I was looking round. This was Pretoria. We had union members in Pretoria, and I thought, I'd like them to see that I'm arrested and I'm in Pretoria. I thought my people thought I was in John Vorster Square and nobody knew where I was.

I was looking round at the street newspaper vendors. All the people selling newspapers in Pretoria would have known that it was me, but it was just not my lucky day. None of our union members did I come across. I knew I wouldn't say anything to them, but at least they would be able to say, 'We saw her in Pretoria. She is still alive.'

There were passers-by. Black, white and all that. They stared, turned their heads. You could hear *'Ag, shame'* from the black people.[1]

We got into this building, a huge building. You could see that it was a government building. It must have been yet another police station within Pretoria. I was taken into another room and the handcuffs were taken off my hands. There was a chair where I sat, and after a few minutes my husband and my sister-in-law came into that room.

This was 23 December. It was about four weeks since I'd seen them. Instead of excitement I felt very dampened. All the hell I had walked through, of those people in that long corridor falling on their knees. All that, and it was for a visit from my husband. And still what I wanted was water, water, water.

Well, then it came, at last, the joy, the excitement. But we were not allowed to speak in our own language. There was a white policeman there who wanted to hear everything we were talking about, and conditions were laid down. You don't ask her about the conditions of her arrest. You don't ask her what she does. You discuss family matters and nothing else.

He hugged me and kissed me, and I don't remember them stopping him, to say 'Don't do that.' And my dear husband had brought a pillow for me. He knew that I needed pillows. I don't know how he thought about it. There was dried fruit, too. There was everything.

And then he said, 'Have you been getting all the things we've been sending you?'

I said, 'No, I haven't received anything.' This was the first time that I'd received something from home, this dried fruit.

He said, 'Well, I'm going to make enquiries.'

I have heard a story about the same thing. A mother was bringing food and clothes for this child who was detained for months. And then one day a black warder said, 'You should stop bringing your child these things. He's been dead for three months.' Can you

---

[1] *'Ag, shame'* is an expression commonly used by white and black South Africans. It means, 'Oh, what a pity.'

imagine? They'd let her come, let her come, when they knew that the child was no more. And to my husband, who was bringing these things every week, they said, 'Once a week on Friday, things are being accepted,' and so he kept bringing them when actually I wasn't receiving these things at all.

Amongst other things that he brought me were Christmas cards, from Bishop Tutu, whom I knew personally, and Leah, his wife, who is a friend of mine, and some from people working with me. And my children had sent Christmas cards from overseas to Tom. He brought these as well, and I said, 'Am I going to be allowed to take these to the cell?' And he told me I was allowed six cards. He had by now begun his work with the Detainees' Parents Support Committee (DPSC), and I have in my keeping a copy of the minutes of the meeting they had with the security forces during which they had bargained for detainees to receive this number of cards. I do not know how they arrived at the figure.[1]

He told me about my children, and I wanted to know, 'What do they think?' and he said they were okay. And I wondered, did my father know that I had not committed any crime, and insisted, 'Tom, please sit my father down and make him understand that I have not committed any crime. I don't know why I am here.'

My next concern was, 'What's going on in the union? Is the union okay, Tom? Is everything okay?' And he made all the assurances that people were working very hard and all was well in the union. He brought greetings from Morris Kagan to say he was very concerned and was doing everything he could to see that the union continued.

It was about fifteen minutes, and this visit was like a lifetime to me. When they were asked to leave the room I wasn't able to cry. I

[1] The DPSC was formed in September 1981, following the spate of detentions that was to lead to Emma's own arrest in November. It monitors and publicises detention figures in South Africa, and its picketing in front of John Vorster Square provoked a new law making it an offence to protest within 500 metres of a law court. Families of detainees are helped by DPSC advice offices in all South Africa's major centres and some small towns, both to establish the whereabouts of those detained and to gain access to them, and to raise funds for legal aid, travel costs and food parcels. Medical treatment and psychological counselling is offered to former detainees and persons injured by security forces in the townships. It was restricted in its activities, effectively banned, in February 1988. For the minutes of the meeting to which Emma refers, see Appendix B.

wasn't even able to cry, and I felt I wasn't going to cry because it would break his heart. Tom is a tall, huge man, and he is a very strong person. He insisted that I've got to be strong, that they would do everything in their power to get me out of that place, but still he couldn't tell me, 'Hey, look here, you're not the only one arrested. There's very many.' He couldn't tell me that. It was just, 'You've got to be strong.'

Back into my handcuffs again, and with the handcuffs I had to cuddle the things he'd brought for me, and a black policeman, another one, had to carry some of the parcels all that long walk back to the car and now back to my cell.

That long corridor I walked now. There were no people. Just that long walk back. But sitting in my cell, looking at those things, having seen my husband for the first time for all those weeks, having heard about how my family was, looking at those cards – I can't explain how I felt. I think it was the greatest day I've ever had.

There came Christmas Day. On Christmas Day I heard the excited women outside bring a plate of food and put it at the door. I could hear them as they walked up and down saying, 'Shame, this food has been lying here for such a long time.' They were jovial. You could feel it was Christmas and everybody was excited, but nobody ever cared that that woman inside had got to eat, and I was looking forward to it, thinking that because it was Christmas it must be nice food.

It was the most disappointing plate of food I've ever seen. By the time they'd shoved it in, to look at it and find that beetroot peel again, the worst thing they gave me – well, I'd just had enough. I had the dried fruit which my husband had brought, and I had my cards which he had brought, too, and I kept on reading those cards and analysing the signatures, reading every word. But from 1982 until this day I no longer can eat dried fruit, because it brings back the memories.

I had my dress and my nightie, but that was all the clothes I had. I had to wash them and hang them in the room. It didn't bother me – I didn't have to leave the room for anything – but maybe this was why I was so cold. I had no business to be so cold in a closed room in Pretoria in mid-summer.

*

After Christmas I began to be taken for exercise. I was taken on top of the roof of that building – right on top of that roof. You just see a valley. And I could see a train, from a very great distance, like a worm moving.

But you could not stand this for long. The top of the building was painted with very bright silver, and it was very hot. The policemen who were my escort were not walking with me. They sat in a place somewhere where there was shelter. I was forced into that sun and glare, but no one could stand to walk with me.

The first day I actually fell to my knees, trembling to stand up, because this light was so bright and I'd been so cold. It was blinding, blinding, this hot sun. They said it was supposed to be thirty minutes' exercise of walking round, but it was so bright you just wanted to go back to the cell.

This happened about three or four times, and I dreaded it. They would not let me come down if I went and said, 'It is enough.' I'd just go and sit on the steps we had come up and hold on to the rail.

In early January there came two black women to the corridor where my cell was. They were going to be executed. I could hear them talking, but they were not sounding angry about going to be hanged. The only time I could hear their anger was when they were angry about my food, which was standing outside the door and was cold, and about the type of food I was eating. But when it came to themselves they were talking sweetly – 'Make me beautiful, so that when I meet with my Creator I am beautiful' – all such things, so much courage.

One day I heard one of these women say to the other, 'Please do my hair smartly, I want to look beautiful when I meet my Maker.' The next day the section was silent. I heard a warder and the other woman talking. The other woman was saying if she had not been pregnant she would have been executed that day, too. She said she was going to name the baby after her friend. I don't know what happened to her, or her baby.

During this period I had, with my headaches and dizziness, a terrible backache. I complained to the nurse to say, 'Your tablets are not giving me any relief from the pain,' and they took me to a doctor. When they X-rayed me I had to go on quite a high machine, and it was an effort. I was so weak I couldn't easily get up there. They said the result showed there was nothing wrong with my back, but it was so painful. The doctor was a very elderly white man, and he didn't concern himself with anything except for the examination. Just that it was not broken. But I still had the pain.

I had been in my cell for two months now. And the days went by. The days went by.

8

Jeppe Police Station

In January I was moved from Pretoria to Johannesburg. Once again I wasn't told anything. It was, 'Pack your things, pack your things and you go.' And I thought perhaps I was going home.

We drove to Johannesburg and to the Jeppe police station.[1] When the car stopped there, I thought perhaps they were collecting somebody or something. Instead I was just told to get out, and there were police sitting in an office, and they started mocking me – 'Yes, such a woman to be in prison. If I was the prime minister I'd kill all the people like yourselves.' All this was said in Afrikaans. Young policemen, saying whatever they wanted to say, laughing at you, and you so nervous and afraid.

Then it was through that office and a gate and yet another gate and into a cell I was shoved. A cell as big as a garage that can accommodate a car. A huge cell, after my very small, clean cell. From my very clean cell with a bed to this dirty place. The walls were dirty. The floor was dirty. There was a bundle of black blankets in the corner, and a bit of carpet, and I was shoved into that place. No bed, no chair, nothing. A lavatory, again filthy. I said, 'Now this is the end of the road. I can't take this.'

There was a window to outside, very high, and from the noise of that other place, with the laundry machines always going, I now had trains, trains, trains. And when those trains were moving it was as if

[1] Jeppe police station is to the east of Johannesburg city centre. Most detainees at this time were held in police stations rather than prisons, and detainees were under the control of the police rather than the prisons department.

the cell was under the railways and the trains were moving over it. I wished I could go back to where I had been. I'd accepted prison, but the conditions here were bad. Very bad.

I would have to sleep on the floor, with my bad back and those black dirty blankets. Yet that evening they brought the food, and it was so lovely. It was very, very good. But I was afraid to eat it. I became suspicious. Why were they giving me such good food? I had not had a proper meal for such a long time, and now when I was given a proper meal I just thought, 'God, are they bribing me to do something or are they bribing me to speak?' Because there had not been any interrogation all along.

So I could not eat the food, and when they came to collect the plate they just found that I had not eaten. This caused concern to them. I ate only the food they brought me in the mornings, their coffee and their bread, but at lunch-times and evenings I would not eat.

I'd lost a lot of weight, during my imprisonment in Pretoria and now I had to visit the dentist on several occasions. I was losing my teeth, I think from the loss of weight and the kind of food I was eating. I was also taken to the doctor, because of my back, and the warder would give me medicine every evening, because I was not allowed to keep the medicine myself.

It was in this way that I discovered I was not alone. One day as they gave me the medicine I was curious with my eyes and read on one bottle the name H. Koornhoff.

I thought, 'Oh, my God, I'm not alone.' There was somebody else here in the prison with me. But so quiet. So silent. You could not hear any movement to say there was a cell next door or whatever.

But I took relief from that, and then when the food kept on being good food the whole time and I would not eat a young white policeman wanted to know, 'Why don't you eat?' And I said, 'Does everyone eat this kind of food?' And he said, 'Yes.'

And then he asked, 'Why are you here?'

This was the first act of kindness. 'Why are you here?'

He spoke English. I said, 'You know why I am here. Why are you asking me why I am here?' And he said, 'Well, I'm only a policeman. I don't know why you're here.'

So I said, 'Why are *you* here?' Because it was unusual for me to see a young white man who spoke in English and treated me like a human being.

He told me that instead of going into the army he chose to be a policeman. He thought it was better to be a policeman than to go into the army. So I thought maybe he was being sincere, even with my suspicion of all these things.

Then also there was a black policewoman who came to check on me – 'Is everything okay?' and so forth.

The first day I just said, 'Yes, yes,' but as the days went by I complained to say, 'Can I have an extra blanket or an extra mat?' meaning just something to make this floor softer. She gave me that. And when I asked her about the food she said everybody ate this kind of food. She said it was the same food, cooked from the same pot as for every other arrested person, black and white. Because I was saying, 'Is it food just for detainees?' And she told me detainees and white persons eat the same food. So I got encouraged and started eating again.

But I was so glad – oh my God, I was so glad to see a black person, even a black police person. I was so sick of seeing those white people. To see always white people, white people pushing your food at you through the door, white people pushing you and telling you 'Come' or 'Go' and what to do – it was making me ill. Because when you are black you have a need for persons of your own colour. And with my envy of white people, now to be surrounded by them made me realise again how stupid that was, to envy their skin or hair. It was no privilege to be among them. It was a misery and a deprivation.

To the doctor I complained time and time again about sleeping on the ground and not having a chair. It meant that all the time I was squatting on the floor. For my age and size, all I had to do was squat. And the doctor said, 'Okay, I will tell them.' I would go for weekly check-ups and each time he would say, 'All right, I'm going to report that you've got to have a chair.' A chair, not a bed.

It was for me an outing, to visit the doctor, or the dentist, even if the reason was pain with my back, or my teeth falling out. And this was how I felt about my interrogation when it began. An outing to get out of my cell.

I was fetched one day in February to go to John Vorster Square from Jeppe, by car. I was manacled again. I soon got used to that. It meant nothing.

And there came now this questioning time.

There could be about four people, at times six people. At times I would stand, at times I would sit, and these people would take turns. This could go on for the whole day. Questioning you about this, questioning you about that. Sometimes they would ask me if I wanted coffee, but I would always ask for water instead. I didn't want to be seen sitting drinking coffee with these people. They would be at one end of the room, with a table. I would be at the far end of the room. They worked in shifts. One shift would go to lunch and leave me with another shift. Once they gave me some lunch, bread and tea, but I wasn't ever hungry there, and anyway when I went back to my cell my plate of food would be there. Maybe that's why they didn't bother to give me any. They knew my food would be waiting for me at the end of the day, and what did I know about lunch-times? I was nothing but a Kaffir. Then, at the end of the questioning, they would just leave me. They wouldn't say goodbye or anything. They would just go, and the next thing would be another policeman coming to say, 'Follow me.' Not to say where to. Just, 'Follow me.'

Even in the car they would play tricks on you and confuse you about where you were going. They would conceal from you any cars coming in or out with other detainees. There would always be a driver, and one policeman next to him with a gun, and two escorts sitting either side of me – all just to take me from prison to prison. The waste of manpower in this! Sometimes it would depress me very much, the waste of these working people, with more education just handed to them than we blacks could get with all our struggles – for what? To sit there in a room learning nothing, doing nothing, always questioning and never understanding what they were being told. It is frightening. Very frightening.

There were times when I would believe them, that with all that manpower I must be a very dangerous person. And then again I would not believe them, but would see that I was helpless, like a child, and that even to go to the toilet was beyond my powers in that room, because I must ask, and wait for permission to be allowed, and then someone must escort me. At first this was very embarrassing for me, but after a time I managed to make myself see that it was the white women warders who should feel humiliated, to have to watch me wipe my bottom.

I was thoroughly questioned about my trade union work. They

weren't interested in the GWU, just in CCAWUSA. And they seemed very interested in the Allied Publishing strike of newspaper workers, which I suppose was really a turning point for us, and showed how strong we had grown. They were also very interested in my relationship with the other leaders who had been arrested before me. At times they would tell me directly that I had been very obstinate and very difficult to the employers. They would remind me of instances, saying, 'Do you remember that this is what you were saying to a certain employer?' One interrogator told me that he was among those people who were talking to me, saying that the workers had to go back to work and that I was being difficult. And sometimes they would leave me and I would hear in another room a tape being played, and I guessed they had recordings of some of the meetings I had been involved with. So it seems that in our industrial relations in South Africa you not only deal with the employers when you negotiate but you deal with the police as well.

Most of them were not intelligent. They were even very stupid. I know I never had the opportunity to complete my education, but they were very stupid, I must say. There was one who had read a lot about trade unions, I think, and one particular man would question me about my friends. What was I doing with Alan Fine, and what was I doing with Neil Aggett, and what was I doing with Barbara Hogan? I knew all these people had been arrested and were in prison. And they were questioning me about our meetings and our trade union centre and where this idea had come from, that somebody must have put this or that idea into my head. They wanted to know if I had ever read certain books – I can't remember the names, because in fact I hadn't read them, but they were Marxist books, because Marxists were the sort of people who have that type of thought, of bringing people together. I was interested in a trade union centre for worker education. Not necessarily with any ulterior motives behind it. But I was interrogated for hours to come up with the truth about the idea and where I got it from.

Always they wanted the truth, when I had no more truth to tell. I don't think they ever really understood that in fact there was nothing to give away. But they always tried to find it, this nothing. They'd make me sit down and write, and perhaps in my writing they wanted me to say things, but there was nothing I could write that would give anybody away, because I'd write about my trade union matters. I would sit and write, and write, and this was better for me. Maybe it was a way of being able to think what to say without for once anyone pushing me and going on – 'Come on, come on, now. Speak.' And being rough about it.

I was never physically abused by them. Just pushed around, but not battered or assaulted. It was an emotional battery, I suppose. There was a woman who would say, 'If you tell the truth and nothing else you will be able to go back to your children in good time'. And then there was a policeman who was very angry and bullying, called Whitehead, who would tell me I was fat, but that I was not to worry because by the time I left this place I would be the size of a marble, I would have lost so much weight. And that I would lose my position with the union, which had made me so hot-headed. And that when I came out my husband would no longer be there.

It was this Whitehead who openly said he was present at one of the meetings where the workers were out on strike, and that he had heard me 'talking back' to the bosses. He was a young man, only in his early thirties I should say, well-built, burly, with a red face. And of all those questioners he is the one I most hated.

I remember one day, as I was on the tenth floor walking up there, I saw the man who was arguing with my husband the day they arrested me. They called him Colonel somebody. And when I saw him I just became very strong and I said to him, 'When are you taking me back to my home, from where you fetched me?' And he said, 'How can I take you back home when your husband says that I brought the books into his house the day when I had come to arrest you?'

I was at times going again to John Vorster Square to meet my husband, but we could not speak of all he was doing outside for me. It was still not allowed. But now I knew that there were still problems continuing about that, and that my husband was still standing firm.

Worst of all was one particular day when I was being driven to John Vorster Square and we were going down Commissioner Street. Out of anxiety I would always look round to see if I could see people I knew. I would see them, but I couldn't wave to them because I was with two policemen, sitting next to me. That day I saw on the posters, 'DETAINEE DIES IN CELL'.

'Detainee dies in cell, detainee dies in cell . . .' And I can't ask these people what has happened or what is going on.

When I got to John Vorster Square my father, my husband, my brother and my sister-in-law were there, and I was excited to see them, but at the back of my mind my concern was for those posters. 'Detainee dies in cell.'

My dad told me, 'I know you will be all right and you will come home, and I know you have not committed any offence. Please be strong.' Everybody always said I must be strong. I wasn't very happy, and I could see my sister-in-law was a bit sad and I didn't want to ask her why. I thought about the detainee who had died in the cell.

When I went back to Jeppe I wanted to know from the policeman, 'I understand there is a detainee who has died in the cell. Who is this detainee?' And one policeman said, 'Okay, I will call you somebody senior who will come in and talk to you.' I think it was a Section 6 inspector who came. And he said, 'I believe you have got a question.' I said, 'Yes, I want to know who is this detainee who has died in the cells.' He said, 'Who told you that? Who told you that?' I said, 'Nobody told me.' He said, 'Where did you get it from?' He was becoming aggressive. I told him I had read the posters at the corner of the street. And he said, 'Can you guess who it is?'

Guessing. How could I guess who it was? He was amused then, smiling and amused.

I started calling names of people who I knew could never have been arrested. I wasn't so stupid as to call the names of persons I knew were in prison. There would be more demands for the 'truth' then, more 'How did you know? Who told you? Tell us the truth.' So I mentioned all the other names and he was very amused. I was like a fool.

He never told me who that person was. And this was a torture and a hell to me. But a few weeks thereafter I went to John Vorster Square again and there was my husband. He was now bringing me fruit juice in five-litre boxes. One time it was peach, orange, apple and so forth. I had these boxes in my cell. When they were empty I kept them. The colour meant much to me – the green, the orange – it was my closeness to nature. It kept me going. It was fun. But then my husband also brought me a transistor radio, which was a gift from my friend David Webster, a founding member of the DPSC who was later assassinated, shot dead by a passenger in a speeding car as he entered his home on 1 May 1989.

He showed me how to put the batteries in, and I was so nervous. I didn't know if this was going to be allowed and he said, 'Look, you must have it.'

I took it back with me. Now I had company. There was music. But also I could listen to the news. And one day when I was listening to the news I just heard the radio say that Australian trade unions refused to offload goods from South Africa because of Neil Aggett's death in detention.[1]

[1] Neil Aggett's death in detention on 5 February 1982 provoked a public outcry, both in South Africa and throughout the world. In the week after he died, over 85,000 workers in hundreds of South African factories downed tools or left the shop floor in a half-hour tribute to him, the first time industrial action of a political nature had been taken on the shop floor rather than in the form of a stay-away. An official police statement claimed he had been found hanging in his cell and that indications were he had committed suicide, a claim Dr Aggett's friends and family, and those who knew about conditions for detainees, found highly improbable. The inquest into his death was delayed by legal arguments about the admissibility of a statement made by Dr Aggett fourteen hours before his death, alleging that he had been assaulted with kicks and punches on 4 January and given electric shock treatment on 29 January.

The fourteenth birthday of Emma's
younger daughter, Penny, 1968. Holding
the cake is Elias, Emma's father.

Penny (holding the child) and Dudu,
Emma's second daughter (second
from right).

Penny at sixteen, not long before her tragic death.

Penny's funeral.

Molly, Emma's eldest daughter, and her husband Aubrey with their two children, just before they left for Germany in 1980. Aubrey was murdered in 1988.

Emma with her husband Tom and daughter Nomsa (actually Tom's daughter, but Emma regards her as *her* child) on Emma's release from detention in May 1982.

Mphoentle (Beautiful Gift), Emma's eldest granddaughter.

Emma with her daughter Molly (second from right) at her friend's graduation party.

Farewell presentation from the Jeppe/ Doornfontein branch of the Garment Workers' Union, 1975.

Emma with Morris Kagan (second from left) at the 19th World Congress of FIET (International Federation of Commercial, Clerical, Professional and Technical Employees) in Caracas, 1979.

Emma was the first South African, and the first woman, to be appointed to the Africa Committee of FIET. Here she is with representatives of Senegal, Ghana, Nigeria, Togo and Egypt at the Nairobi meeting of the Committee.

CCAWUSA's Executive Committee, with Emma at the head of the table (second from right) meets with FIET delegates in Johannesburg in 1984. Alan Fine is fourth from right.

Emma, as General Secretary of CCAWUSA, addresses striking 'Pick 'n' Pay' hypermarket workers (above) and Central News Agency (CNA) workers (below).

At a Sharpeville Massacre commemorative meeting in 1988. Together with residents of Sharpeville are Leah Tutu (fourth from left) and Emma (third from right).

Khotso House after the bomb in 1988.

At Khotso House in 1988.

Emma Mashinini (left) and Joyce Seroke at an impromptu demonstration in Soweto against the conferring of the 'Freedom of Soweto' by the collaborationist Soweto Council on Dr Piet Koornhof, Minister of 'Plural Relationships and Development', in 1980. The demonstrators were attacked with tear gas and rubber bullets, just as the Minister's helicopter flew low over their heads. To the delight of the crowd, he could be seen with his handkerchief over his face, victim of his own tear gas. He had to abandon the attempt to land, and never received the honour planned for him.

9

Dudu

' . . . Australian trade unions are refusing to offload . . . because of the death in detention of . . .' They said the name and then they linked to say he was a trade unionist. I waited for a few hours and then the news came again and they said it again. I still did not believe what I had heard. I got such a shock. Here was I, all by myself, and I couldn't tell anyone about the death of my friend.

It was stale, old news. It was weeks since I'd seen those posters, very many weeks. When I questioned the white police who brought the food, saying, 'Is it true that Neil Aggett has died?' they said, 'I don't know.' And then I spoke to the black policeman and said, 'Is it true?' and he said, 'Yes. It is true.' I questioned the black policewoman and the black policeman, and they said, 'Okay, we'll try and see if we can get the newspapers.'

The first cuttings they brought me were from an Afrikaans newspaper. There was a picture of Neil and the name, but I could not pretend to understand what had happened. So I asked if I could see the *Rand Daily Mail* and they said, 'Okay, we'll try.'

So now they were bringing me the *Rand Daily Mail* concealed in their clothing. They'd walk into my cell, and speak to me, and then they would just pass on the newspaper to me. It was great joy to read it. I'd read every bit, but I had to be careful. In Pretoria I'd never have been able to do it, but this window was so high nobody could see me through it. They had to actually come in, through the door, and I could hear them, with the keys jangling. I'd read the newspaper and then hide it under the mat. And when I'd read the newspaper I'd tear it into little pieces, then flush it.

In the newspapers I read about the people who were admitted to hospital. I read that somebody from the South African and Allied Workers' Union (SAAWU) was taken in for psychiatric treatment, and that Liz Floyd, Neil Aggett's girlfriend, had been admitted to the general hospital. And I started realising that there were many of us inside here. It made me feel braver. I all of a sudden just gained strength.

I asked at this time for things to clean the place. I was given disinfectant for the toilet, and I cleaned the walls and the floor. It was interesting cleaning the walls, because in places I could read, 'I WAS HERE FOR RAPE', and a signature, or 'I WAS HERE FOR STEALING CARS'. Everybody who had been in that cell wrote on that wall what they were there for, and it kept me busy, reading all this. But then it began to torture me, because I thought that I was not a criminal. Why must I be sitting in a cell of rapists and people who stole cars and who were selling liquor? So I washed the walls as far as I could, and my toilet was now nice and clean, and again and again I'd pour the disinfectant into it.

Now every day when they came with their loud keys to open up, I would be there with my beautiful colours and big bright bath towel which also gave colour to the whole. And now they also started taking an interest in this particular lady criminal who was so concerned about being tidy in her room, although when I wanted hot water for the hot-water bottle my husband sent me because I had cold feet, they said I should get my hot water from the tap. No tap water is hot enough, but they told me I was not in the Carlton Hotel. Only on some days could I get really hot water, and then it was a privilege.

But under all this was Neil Aggett. His death affected me very deeply. We were very close friends with this man.

I would remember when Alan Fine was detained and Neil Aggett came to take his place in my life. He used to visit my office every day to enquire, 'Is there anything I can do?' I was very concerned about Alan Fine, because I like him dearly, and I knew Neil Aggett did too. I couldn't visit him. All I could do was call his mother to find out how he was and she would always tell me, 'He's okay.'

Neil was the first white person to die in detention. He had his profession as a doctor, which he could have concentrated on safely, without ever getting himself involved in trade union work. He was supposed to have killed himself, but everybody who dies in detention is supposed to have killed himself. I don't know what they find to kill themselves with in those cells. There was no chair for me, not even to burn myself to death.

The police hated that white people should work for justice for black people. When they interrogated me they didn't know I had found out that Neil Aggett was dead. They would time and time again tell me, 'We're going to question him about this.' I remember Whitehead would use very vulgar words when he spoke about Neil. I could see he was furious and mad about him, that there was no more price that Neil could pay, because he had died on them. And in fact it was this man who was questioned about Neil's death, and as a result was demoted from the security forces and made a policeman, working in the robbery squad.[1] He was mad about Liz and Liz, too: Liz Thompson and Liz Floyd.

Strangely, I was not made more frightened when I went in for my interrogation. Instead I was furious about the whole thing. I was sort of arguing back. I started kicking out to say, 'I'm not going to be questioned about things I don't know.' I'm a very well travelled person, and when I was questioned about my travels I would say whatever I wanted to say because my travels were genuine. It wasn't to plan for people to come and take over the workers, or whatever it was they thought.

I was still getting the newspapers, and one thing really gave me a lot of pride when I saw it. There was a cutting with a photograph of my husband standing as a lone demonstrator in front of the Supreme Court, demanding my release. Tom standing there, alone, with a placard, demanding. And I read about him even coming to Cape Town and demanding my release, and demanding the release of all the other detainees.

The main important thing they were saying was, 'Why are they not being charged?' They insisted we had to be charged, rather than be kept in prison all this time. And he was arguing that he knew of no offence that I'd committed, and that it seemed I'd been arrested for my trade union work. And these people kept saying I wasn't arrested for my trade union work, but for being a political activist. And the big

---

[1]Officially, no one was found guilty of Neil Aggett's death. The verdict at the inquest was suicide.

thing was that Tom seemed to be negotiating as an equal, and did not feel any intimidation. His first act the day they detained me had been to refuse to sign for the books that they were removing from my house, and this was sufficient to prove that Tom was a very strong and conscientious person. But he was not one to speak out. My being detained, him demonstrating in front of the Supreme Court, the police station, demanding my release and going to Cape Town to demand my release there – this Tom was a person who spoke out, which he hadn't been before. So sometimes when the police think they're doing you down, they're building you up. They built me up by harassing me in front of the shopworkers, and helped make the union what it is. And they made my husband speak out, so that today if the police knocked on the door I would look around to say, 'Who are they after?' – unlike before, when I would always think it was me.

When it came to Easter, because I am a staunch member of the Anglican Church, I made my demands during the interrogation to say that I wanted to receive Holy Communion.

Tom had brought me a Bible to read in my cell, and also other reading material, little novels with love stories. I also saw someone from my Be United group, who brought me a dress and warm underwear, because it was winter, and said that all the underwear was from money collected by the Be United group.[1] And any particular day when I had visitors I told them that I wanted to have Bishop Tutu come and give me Holy Communion. I said this openly in front of the police, and the police said that, much as they would look into my demand to receive Holy Communion, I was not to think they would have Bishop Tutu coming into their offices.

I went on, though. I really insisted on having Bishop Tutu and Holy Communion. Even the Section 6 inspector who had religiously been coming to visit me every second week heard about it. Now, for the first time, I was making my demands. I was demanding Bishop Tutu and Holy Communion.

When Good Friday came I was fetched from the cell and taken to

[1]Be United is an all-women group made up of friends and colleagues who act as a *stokvel* but also meet to discuss politics and other matters of interest and concern.

John Vorster Square. And instead of going to the tenth floor, where I was usually taken, I was taken to the ninth floor. I was surprised and worried by even this small change. The lack of communication is one of the worst things – whatever happens, even if it is a good thing, it is not communicated to you, so you never know what is going on. You are just left to fall back on your own anxieties and fears.

But I had a very good day. As I was going to the ninth floor, where I saw several men with handcuffs, and was saying to myself, 'Am I going to be tortured together with these men?' a young man came walking down the steps as we were coming up. He noticed me, and he just said, 'Don't be so morose.' And he kissed me. He had his escorts, but he braved them to speak to me and then to kiss me. His name was Sisa Njikelana,[1] and I carried his kiss with me for a very long time. When people speak about the kiss of life, I tell them that kiss of Sisa Njikelana was a kiss of life to me. He was such a young man – young enough to be my son – but he put life into me.

When we reached the ninth floor we went into a room and I found my priest there, Father Telejani, from the Holy Cross in Soweto. When I was demanding Bishop Tutu and Holy Communion they had suggested other Anglican priests, whom I had totally refused. So I don't know what happened or how they ended up with Father Telejani – maybe they found out he was my priest in Soweto and so brought him. He is a very intelligent man, but he never used to preach about politics, about the real things. Human rights.

So in that room were Father Telejani, the two police and myself. And the table. He had prepared the table exactly as he would in church. He had everything necessary. He had the wines, he had the little jars, and he was in full cassock, in full attire.

I was excited to see him, and I kissed him, and that was allowed, and he sang a hymn, 'Praise to the Holiest'. And after that he made his prayers. As we were singing you could hear the police join in with humming, because they would not leave me alone with my priest. And when it was time to say 'Amen' you could hear them say 'Amen', and I thought how, with all the horrible things that happen in South Africa, this was still meant to be a Christian country.

---

[1] Sisa Njikelana was the Vice-President of the SAAWU. He was detained on 8 December 1981, and on several other occasions, charged, under the Terrorism Act. Two years ago he was paralysed in a motor accident.

So then the priest brought me greetings from the Church, and I gave him greetings to the Church, and we hugged and we kissed, and it was wonderful.

Afterwards, as I was walking back to my cell, I was walking very tall. I had been given a Bible. This Bible was from Bishop Tutu as a gift to me. So now I had two Bibles. And when we got downstairs into the basement from the ninth floor Sisa Njikelana was there, and he was followed by two white young ladies who were waving goodbye to him.

His home was in the Eastern Cape, so when I saw that he had visitors I was glad that there were people from around Johannesburg who would visit him. And downstairs when I was in the car I saw these young ladies again and stupidly I opened the door to say to them, 'Thank you for visiting Sisa.' And just then a senior policeman went past and saw me speaking to these girls, and the person who was driving the car was taken to task because it was said he had purposely allowed me to talk to those people. It was worse because his name was Mashinini. He was no relation, but when I came out of detention we met and he told me about the trouble he had got into for speaking to me. But I wanted to convey to these two young girls that I was very grateful that at least they were visiting this young man, even if his family was too far away. And the girls spoke to me and knew me, even though I didn't know them. They were saying, 'Emma, keep strong, keep strong, you are going to come back, you are going to come back.' They were shouting very loudly. To this day I don't know who they were.

Another time, when I was visiting the doctor, there was a prisoner next to me, and I said to him, 'Hello, I know who you are, but I don't know your name.'

This was Frank Chikane, a priest who has been arrested on several occasions. He's out now, but he's in and out of prison.[1] We had quite an interesting conversation. I said, 'Who are you? What are you doing here?' And he just said, 'I was arrested at the same time as you.' I think he was with very many others in his cell – too many – and they were able to converse and pass on what was going on. It was more rare for women to be arrested, and I think more white women than

[1] Frank Chikane is now the General Secretary of the South African Council of Churches.

black women were arrested at this time, so when I went to Pretoria I was the only black woman there. But Frank Chikane was able to give me news.

Another day I was sitting there waiting for the doctor and I saw a woman come in. She looked so different to me, but I knew her face. This was Liz Thompson, the friend of Neil Aggett's girlfriend, Liz Floyd. She waved at me, and when she waved at me I think the police saw and so they moved us to another place. They wanted no contact between me and people.

These outings – to the doctor, to the interrogation, to my visitors – served a very good purpose, because it was going out to meet people, to see other things and most of all to see people. Even interrogation I looked forward to. And if they didn't call me for interrogation, I really wanted to remind them, because interrogation was better than to be isolated and all by myself for all those months. I even thanked myself for being so ill, because of the outings to the doctor and the dentist. The doctor I was now seeing for my backache was a Jewish doctor, and was very friendly. He promised me a chair every time but the chair never came. And he'd talk about my illness and the names of the tablets and so on. My back, you see, was aching all along, and I was experiencing what they call hot flushes. I would feel very warm suddenly, and then I'd perspire and it would leave me. I'd heard people speaking about hot flushes but I hadn't known what they were. I was fifty-one, and my diet was all wrong.

I had the Bible to read, and the stories my husband had brought me, and the radio, newspapers which I would have to destroy when I'd read them; so much more than at first when it was just me. But somehow the thing that should have brought me the most happiness instead brought me the most pain.

I had a picture of my grandchildren. I was excited to see this the first time. It came out of the books my husband brought me. But afterwards when I looked at the picture it seemed as though those children were talking to me and saying, 'Granny, what are you doing here?' You know what it is to be a grandmother. It's a very important thing. I became very anxious and I was ashamed to look at that picture. I put it right underneath the blankets and slept on top of it, and when I did that it was as though I was squeezing the life out of my own grandchildren. I just did not have anywhere to hide them. I didn't want to destroy this picture, but at the same time I didn't want to look at it because it hurt me. Their eyes were so pressing, as though asking me what I was doing there. And I was thinking about my family day in, day out. I didn't know what my children were doing or what they were thinking about this whole thing. They must be wishing for me to come home.

One day, thinking about my own children – Molly, who was in Germany, my grandchildren, and Dudu who was in New York – thinking about their faces, and putting names to them, I could see my youngest daughter's face and I wanted to call her by her name. I struggled to call out the name, the name I always called her, and I just could not recall what the name was. I struggled and struggled. I would fall down and actually weep with the effort of remembering the name of my daughter. I'd try and sleep on it, wake up. I'd go without eating, because this pain of not being able to remember the name of my daughter was the greatest I've ever had. And then, on the day when I actually did come across the name – this simple name Dudu, or 'Love' – I immediately fell asleep, because it was such a great relief. But that was after days of killing myself to remember my own child's name.

I did not know anything about the psychological effects of trauma. These are things I've only learnt about since coming out of hospital. I thought instead that I was going mad. Really going mad. And I was fighting very much against it because now I could read in the newspapers that people were going into psychiatric hospitals and I didn't understand that you could go mad from being arrested. I just thought I was sick.

It's only now, after years, that I feel I want to speak about this effect of being in detention. Not to talk about it is to deprive a number of people who will come up against it for the first time without knowing what their expectations should be. So it's the first time for everybody, and this is what the system wants. The day I was released I was told, 'You mustn't discuss your detention with anybody,' and I was obedient. I was afraid to speak about it in case it would leak. I did not want to go back where I had been.

After visits from my family or friends I felt restored. It gave me more strength than ever before. So you can imagine what happens to people who do not have anyone to visit them. I think this was why I went so wild and excited to see those two young ladies who had come to visit Sisa. But with that there was the guilt. There was a song which was sung on the transistor – 'Every time you go away, just take a little bit of me with you . . .' Something of that nature. And I thought, I've been going away all my life. I'm a traveller. I'm always going away and now here I am in prison. It means again I have found myself to be a nuisance in my family. I'm always causing them pain by going away. All I could hope was they understood that I had not committed any crime. I hoped I had not done anything to offend them. I worried about my friends. I thought, Are they going to receive me when I come back?

So in prison you are anxious and concerned about everything. You are killing yourself about being there and what's going to happen tomorrow, and all that, and you look forward to your outings – to the doctor, to visitors, and to the interrogations.

And then, one day, the interrogations just stopped. That was it – bang. No word. Nothing about why. And I missed them. I thought once again I was going to be sitting in that room all by myself. I didn't think I knew myself any longer. There was no mirror. It's odd what happens when you don't see yourself in a mirror for such a long time. You don't recognise yourself. You think, who am I? All I had to recognise was a jersey which was sent to me by a friend. It was her jersey and I could recognise it. But I didn't know any longer how to recognise myself.

10

A Kind of Freedom

One morning in May a chair was brought to my cell, so the doctor's orders were at last complied with. I had a chair. But I had not sat on that chair for too long when there was a knock on the door to say, 'Pack your things. Come with us.'

This wasn't anything new for me, to bring my things for interrogation. But I had not had any interrogation for so long, I just thought it was a change from one prison to another again. Leaving that chair behind, that chair which I'd waited so long for, I thought, 'Oh, my God, I'm going to start life all over again without a chair.' The cruelty of people. The cruelty of that chair. I ached. My back ached. I needed that chair.

I was taken to John Vorster Square with all my things, into that office, and in that office I was made to sign papers to say that I would appear in court on a certain day. I don't know what the charges were, and I never did appear in court. It was just a further threat to leave hanging over me. But I did attach my signature, and I was given my things back. My rings, my watch, everything. Only my gold necklace which my daughters bought for me for my fiftieth birthday was not there. I said I wanted my necklace amongst my things, and that it was not there. They said they were going to find that necklace, but they never did. Then an officer made me sign very many more papers. And still I thought I was being transferred to another prison, and stripped again of all my things. It was only after signing all those papers and after being made to make oaths about not talking about being in prison that I realised, 'Oh, I'm being released.'

Then they said, 'How are you going home?'

I asked if I could please phone my husband, to tell him that I was being released. They knew the number. Of course. They knew everything about my husband, and myself. During the interrogation they used to tell me about my husband and myself. They rang him and told him that I was released from prison.

We went down into the basement and out with all my things, and I was left alone at the gate.

While I was down there I met another trade unionist, the Organising Secretary of the GAWU, Rita Ndzanga. I said, 'Rita, have you been here all the time?' She said, 'Yes, I've been here all the time.'

She was totally disorientated. Totally. But I felt very normal – just wildly excited. I wanted to wave to everybody I saw. I was quite normal, and I wanted to speak to people.

It was not long before my husband came. He came accompanied by a friend, Athol Margolis, who was in the National Union of Garment Workers with him. And Athol Margolis jumped in the air because he was so excited.

We gave Rita a lift. First we took Athol back to the union office, to drop him there, and then we went to Soweto.

This was another of the evils of detention. Rita Ndzanga could not find her way home. We drove round and round but Rita could not find where she lived. She knew it was in Senaone, and Tom said if he took her to the station next to there we could trace how she usually came from work. He was asking her, 'You get off from this station, and which route do you take out? How do you go?' But Rita still could not find her home. The next best thing Tom could do was to go to the superintendent's office where we pay rent to say, 'Can you please find the number of the Ndzangas' home,' and when they gave the number and they gave the direction, only then did we manage to take Rita home. She herself then said, 'Oh yes, this is my home,' and the children came out to greet her.

Just as she was about to leave the car, Tom said, 'Emma, where's your mohair blanket?'

I said, 'I don't know, it's at home,' and he said, 'No, this blanket, Emma, I've long sent it to you. Long ago. This is the blanket I thought you had.'

And all along, some of those things he had sent me had gone to the wrong prison, so my blanket had kept Rita warm all the time, and not me. Only just then did I get my blanket back.

Rita was older than me, and she was so traumatised. Once before she had been detained, and her husband also. But her husband had died in detention while she was still being held. He was buried without her being present, and when she came out of detention she went only to a grave. That was in 1977. I remember there was a picture of her in the newspapers, kneeling and praying at the grave of her husband. Just a few years earlier on. And now she had been in detention again. But I am pleased to say she is recovered now, and is still going strong.

So now it was time for me to go home. It was so exciting. My child Nomsa was there, and my neighbours. My neighbours came in very great numbers, and there was one visit especially which was very important to me. Morris Kagan, who until that time had never been to Soweto, came to my house. He said – it was before the permits were abolished – 'Permit or no permit, I'm going to Soweto. I'm going to see Emma.' All this was very wonderful, but also too much, because in the evening, when I went to bed, I was very exhausted from being alone for so long and then all of a sudden having so many people coming.

At night the cars driving back and forth seemed to me now to be interrogators. Every time there was a car I was terrified, and thought that they were coming back to collect me. These people know what they do when they lock you up. You torture yourself.

So the excitement was short-lived. I now had a period when I was very concerned and worried and wanted to run away from my home. My home was no longer suitable for accommodating me safely, because they knew where it was and I thought they were coming back to get me.

We called the doctor, and he gave me something to put me to rest, to sleep. But still that feeling went on, for days and days. And all the time people were coming to see me. They were coming in their tens, in their hundreds. We actually had to have arrangements to say which people were going to visit on a certain day. People from trade unions, people from the Church, from prayer meetings. It was just traffic, one after another. And international friends. I was one of those lucky people who had a telephone in the home, and all the time there were telephone calls from all angles.

I'm sure people could tell from my speech that I wasn't normal. And in the end my FIET colleagues in Geneva said, 'We want you to come to Geneva, and we are prepared for you to travel with your husband. We are not going to take the risk of you travelling alone.'

In May I was out of prison, and now in June I was to travel to Geneva. And from Geneva I was whisked away to go to Denmark, to a clinic for detainees and people who had been tortured.

In Denmark I was given the most royal treatment one could expect. I had wonderful doctors who paid the most important attention to me, I had a ward which was like a suite, I had everything I wanted.

But to me it was yet another detention. Tom had to leave me there, and he went to Germany to spend a few days with the children and then went back to South Africa. And mostly I just felt I'd been away from my family for too long, and now again I was away from my family. So in spite of all the good work that was done by this clinic – the good work which I appreciated very much – the fact remains that I wanted to be with my family again. I think this was bad timing, for me to go to that clinic then. I think, for all their good treatment, it was another disorientation.

I was with other people who were torture victims, coming from other countries. We could not speak because we knew different languages. Only the doctors and nurses could come and speak to me. And when you look at these people who are themselves tortured and derailed, it does not give much courage. It just put me off.

There were mostly men, from Chile, South American men. Some of them had brought their families with them. You could see their wives and children, and there was a lot of unpleasantness. These husbands had been away from home in prison, where they were derailed, and they were different people now – they were not who they had been. There must be unpleasantness in such a circumstance. So these families did not come excited. There was misery all around.

The doctors there were very nice. I remember they tried to keep my presence a secret, so that it would not be known in South Africa that I was having this treatment. They didn't want to use my real name. They wanted to give me a name to cover up who I was. This I refused. It was important to me that I had come and that my name was Emma Mashinini. I wanted to go down on record. This was very important. I wasn't going to accept another name.

The doctor who started the clinic was Inge Genefke, a woman

about ten or twelve years younger than myself, and a very brave, intelligent person. She said the idea had come to her with the aid and help of another woman, who was in Paris. When I was there the clinic was still in a hospital, in a separate wing. But they were building a separate hospital for torture victims.

Inge Genefke used to want me to speak out, to tell her what happened during the whole time of my imprisonment and what the torture was. I had to dig it out. I forgot some of the things, but she was so patient. She wanted me to dig and dig and speak about everything.

But for me I was speaking to a white doctor, and I had spent so much time with white police, surrounded by white people. It was a white woman who had refused me chewing gum, and a white woman who had put those bracelets on me. And it was hard, very hard, to trust her, this new white woman. As well as that, I had been told when I was released never, *never* to speak about my detention. So whenever I spoke I was leaving something out. I was fearful, terribly fearful, that this would leak out and get to them, and I would be rearrested and charged for having spoken about things.

Then the newspapers found out I was in that hospital, and again I had that fear of being betrayed and that the people who said they were helping me would hand me over and return me to prison. The journalist who most hounded me was black. His name was Z.B. Molefe, and he printed an article on 18 July 1982 in the *Golden City Press* in Johannesburg under the headline: 'MYSTERY OF SICK EMMA':

Mystery deepened this week about the whereabouts of prominent trade unionist Mrs Emma Mashinini who is reported to be sick in an overseas hospital.

This was after GCP, assisted by the International Red Cross, contacted more than 30 hospitals in Copenhagen, Denmark – where Mrs Mashinini is reported to be hospitalised – but failed to locate her.

The search for Mrs Mashinini was started after this newspaper published a story on July 4 about her hospitalisation in Copenhagen . . . suffering from what her doctors described as the 'effects of psychological torture' . . .

Mr Mashinini said: 'Her doctors said she was highly affected by her detention.

'They also added that a person who has been physically tortured is better off than a person who has been psychologically tortured . . .'

The mystery of Mrs Mashinini's hospitalisation first surfaced when GCP approached her husband on latest developments.

A nervous Mr Mashinini flatly refused to discuss the matter. Finally he told this reporter: 'You are newspaper people, surely you can find out for yourselves. You have many contacts abroad.'

When I tried to approach Mrs Mashinini's trade union, the Commercial, Catering and Allied Workers' Union, I also met with stony silence.

Said one source at the union's Johannesburg headquarters: 'Sorry, we have been sworn to silence on the matter.'

Again efforts by the London-based headquarters of Amnesty International working together with GCP drew a blank. The next step in this catalogue of mystery was the Danish Trade Union Federation in Copenhagen.

After hours of transcontinental phone calls, a certain nervous Mr Carlsen, said: 'No, no I know nothing about her latest whereabouts. She was long discharged from hospital. I think she is out of the country by now.'

The Danish church organisation, Dan Churchaid, knew nothing about Mrs Mashinini's illness or hospitalisation.

Another influential European labour organisation which knew nothing about Mrs Mashinini's hospitalisation was the Geneva-based International Federation of Commercial Workers.

Back in Johannesburg our search took on the proportions of a mystery detective novel.

Trade union sources revealed to GCP that information about Mrs Mashinini's illness has been shrouded in mystery because 'the family perhaps fears for her life after all she has gone through.' . . .

It was as a result of this that I had to assume my code-name in the hospital. I became Mrs Akhaya, and special security arrangements were made for me. The nurses were instructed not to allow any strange visitors to my bedside. Back at home Tom protested vehemently with Mr Molefe about this intrusion into my private life and the threat he was causing to my safety.

But despite all this I did manage to speak out. I did manage to trust Inge and tell her about my greatest concern, which was that Alan Fine, who was still in prison, would be charged with some offence and that I would be called as a state witness. This sent me totally berserk, to think of being a state witness. So I told her this, and she asked me, 'Why are you so concerned or afraid of being a state witness?' And I said, 'It's because the community can never accept you having been a state witness.' And she was educating me, saying, 'You know that at times people are made state witnesses very much against their will, and they may have broken down, or there may be other very good reasons why they have eventually gone to become a state witness.' After all the trauma, to go back to the community and be rejected again. It means you are killing this person twice over.

Always she wanted me to dig and speak out, and she seemed to enjoy it when I cried. She even laughed when, after all that time of being unable to cry, I did begin to weep. She would just leave me to cry, and she sat and enjoyed it. I didn't at first understand why this was. I didn't understand why she was enjoying something that made me feel so ashamed. I thought that by crying it showed I was weak, and I was humiliated.

She would say, 'Why are you so apologetic? You live for other people. You don't live for yourself. It is important, you've got to think about yourself before you think about the next person.' She would say, 'You've got to be selfish about yourself.'

I was giving her examples to say that yes, I thought I was a selfish person. I said I was a person who could stand up and speak for herself. She said, 'Give me one good example.' And I gave her an example to say that when I wanted to buy a car I had refused to use my husband's name. According to the rules and regulations in South Africa, if you buy a car under hire purchase you have to use your husband's name. But I refused to use my husband's name and said this was my car and therefore it had to be in my name. And I insisted on this until the car dealer really did give in and said it would be in my name, even though it was not supposed to be so. And my husband gave me his support in that. He said, 'Do what you want to do.'

Well, I told her that example. But she said to me, 'That's not enough. That's not being selfish. That is standing up for your rights.'

I tried everything to prove that I can be selfish, and I did not find one thing. And this was a lecture she gave me time and time again: 'Be selfish about yourself. Be selfish. Live for yourself. Stop thinking about other people.'

I try to, but I have not managed to get to that.

1 left Denmark prematurely, I know. Inge felt I should stay longer, but I couldn't. I really was longing to be out of hospital and to go back to my family.

From there I went to join Molly in Germany, and I spent about two weeks with her. This made me feel very good, to be with my daughter, my grandchildren and my son-in-law. Only Dudu I had not seen, although I spoke to her on the phone when I was in Geneva, and the craving to see her was greater than ever.

I remember when I first went from Denmark to Germany to see Molly, when I came out of that hospital, I feared for my life. And when I got to Frankfurt airport to fly home again I looked around and saw two South Africans, Dan Vaughan, the assistant of Desmond Tutu, and Allan Boesak, who is now the Chairman of the World Alliance of Reformed Churches. I don't know where they had come from, but they too were travelling to South Africa and we were going to be on the same plane. This gave me great relief, to know that when I got to the airport there would be someone to say, 'We saw her. We were with her.' So I said to them, 'Thank you. I didn't even need to talk to you. It was just a great relief that I saw you.' And they said, 'This does not happen to you alone. It happens to all of us. After our trips, when we go back home, we wonder what is going to happen to us.'

I am sure people are going to die from heart failure, worrying about getting to that airport at Jan Smuts. There is nothing to hide, nothing, but with the thought that people just disappear between airports the joy of going back to your own country escapes you. Only when you get out of that hole – Jan Smuts airport, Customs – do you feel like saying, 'Free, free, free at last!'

Very many people asked me, when I was in Denmark, why I was going back to South Africa. They said I was in a unique position. My children were out of the country. The only person to come and join me would be my husband. And they would say, 'Don't go back to South Africa.'

But I would say, 'I must go back.' And my children felt, 'If you die, your grave is not going to be in Europe. If you must die, your grave has got to be in Africa. It has to be in South Africa.' Because this is my country. They say, 'We are not here to stay ourselves. We've come to Europe to study, and then we'll go back home. And you must go back home. It's vital. We love you.'

So I had to come back home.

Molly was very homesick in Germany, and wanted to go home very badly, but her husband was not ready. So they actually left him behind, for him to come on after. She wanted to come back to this apartheid country, after Germany where they didn't feel their colour. My grandchild in Germany would call every elderly woman she saw in the street her grandmother, her *Ouma*, and every woman in that whole place knew her. And I was concerned, thinking, What's going to happen when she gets to South Africa? But when she got here it just faded off. I've never heard anybody saying that she's stopped anybody to say, 'It's *Ouma*.' And I think it's because those Germans had ready, smiling faces which attracted her, which has not happened here.

Dudu wants to come home also. When she has finished her training in New York she will come. And now whenever I go to visit her I make my journey back with extra heavy luggage because she is forever giving me her things to bring home. I'm always travelling with two suitcases because all her things must come home. That's sufficient to show that when she has finished her training in business administration – when she has finished training to be a capitalist! – my Dudu will come back to South Africa.

I know, though, that both my children were affected by my detention. It's strange. I thought my elder daughter, Molly, was the weaker, and that Dudu was the one that was strong. But Dudu tells me that in her school in New York they were giving lectures in psychological effects. She said, 'Mum, I could just see you,' and it affected her very badly. I have a letter from her from about this time, shortly after I was released, where she explains what she was going through:

Dearest Mama,

Greetings! I know you should be wondering what is happening with me for not writing as early as I promised. It is really hard to explain, especially in writing. All the same, I will try, and hope you will understand. After speaking to you on the phone I really became sick mentally. I could not explain to anybody what was wrong with me, but there was something wrong. All the same I have now overcome everything. I think I am now fine.

I have just finished writing my final exams, last week Friday. I hope that I have done all right. About my life in the United States, I really have a lot to tell you, but I do not think that it is time for you to be informed at this present moment. You really need to rest, physically and mentally. Time will come when I will have to explain everything in detail.

Please do not worry a lot, as every person has to go through rough life some time or another. It is just unfortunate that you had to experience such during our absence and at the same time I had to undergo all this when I am so far from home. I wish to know more about yourself. I think that is the most important thing at this present moment . . .

. . . I hope you are still at home and having a rest. If I were home I could see to it that you stay at home for at least a month . . .

Mamane with Love . . .

But Molly, who I always thought was the weaker, was very strong. She went from pillar to post for me, and they always told her, 'Your mother is arrested for her political activities.' She even went to the South African Embassy in Germany, where she was told that I was in prison because I was a Communist.

But the love those children showed to me! I think back to how I never had time to love them, to show them, to physically show them that love, and then I look at the love they show to me, and I know it must have been there, and they noticed it in me, and I am so thankful.

So many people were fighting for me when I was detained. And so many people gave me support when I was released. It was not just Tom, and Molly, and Dudu, and my third daughter, Nomsa, who is not really my daughter but Tom's, although she would be very offended if she were to hear me say she was my stepdaughter, because I regard and love her in every way as my daughter. She keeps my home going for me in all my travels. I come back depressed, and Nomsa is there to receive me, to make me happy. She gets up very early to try and clean each and every corner of that home so that when mom comes everything is superbly clean. And most of all, when I came back from detention and I was sickly and disturbed, it was Nomsa who was there with me, for any ailment. For my pleasures, for my disappointments, for my successes and failures, Nomsa has always been there. If I'm a bit on the upset side she wants to know, 'Mom, why don't you invite your friends?' She likes to see us being jolly and happy. She stands in the kitchen all the evening and seems to enjoy it. My fear is that by the time she raises her own family she will be exhausted, and all because of my hundred and one travels.

And as well as all these supporters, there were my colleagues, and all the trade union movement, all over the world. There were the Australian trade unions who refused to offload goods because of Neil Aggett's death, and then, while I was in Geneva, the two international trade secretariats our union is involved with showed me copies of letters which were sent to P.W. Botha – stacks and stacks of letters from different unions, all written to demand my release from prison. There was one letter which was very interesting. It came from the New Zealand hotel workers, and said that when the South African rugby players had come to play in New Zealand they had not known that 'our sister Emma' was imprisoned, and that had they known I was unlawfully arrested the South African players would have had to sleep in their rugby grounds because they would not have found a hotel to accommodate them.

And then there were all my friends, who were all so strong for me and who worked so hard to make me see that I was still a person whom they accepted, despite all my fears and shame at having been a prisoner.

And then there was my car, which was waiting for me when I was ready to drive again.

This car is something I in a way inherited from my mother. She loved beautiful things, and so do I. She was a dressmaker, and very petite, and always wore high-heeled shoes. She was especially a great lover of crystal glass, and so am I.

So I like to think it is for this reason – this love of beautiful things – that I have one special possession – a BMW. I wanted it because it is beautiful, and also, I think, because I have been so deprived of beauty. Deprivation does a lot to a person. The more you are deprived, the more you are envious of things. So I will be paying the hire purchase on my BMW for ever, although – and it is always very ugly to say that detention has done something for me – when I was detained the union paid me my salary for that six months, and all I asked them to do was to take my salary and keep on paying the hire purchase. If I had been around, it would have taken much longer to pay it off. I didn't need the money, where I was. I had my lousy food, my white servants, my white accommodation, my white disturbers at night opening the door, my white manacles, my bed which was the concrete floor. I had all this, and I had the privilege of not being made to pay for it. So all that has gone into my BMW, and I must say that it is a good car. I don't think a cheaper car would have given me the same service. All my friends who have not bought expensive cars have had to change them again and again, and I still have mine.

So it was thanks to all this – my friends and family, psychotherapy, and my beautiful car – that I kept going for those last five years in CCAWUSA. And I needed them, because now that I was beginning to be on the mend there was work for me to do. The union had been going well, but there were many problems – workers in many of the stores were involved in big strikes. CCAWUSA was in a good position to win recognition from many of the companies we dealt with, and I wanted to be there, leading the struggle for workers' rights. I was still at the head of my union.

11

Just a Tiny Giant

The doctors told me I should work half-days, or at the most a four-day week, but it was simply not possible. 1982, of all years, was an important one for CCAWUSA. That was the year we made the retailing employers accept that we were here to stay. It wasn't easy. It took strikes at four of the big employers. They were not all triggered by demands for talks on recognition, but that was always the main issue that would emerge during our talks.

The first big strike was at the Edgars clothing chain group, and it began in May, when I was still in prison. It lasted for about two weeks, and one of the first things I did when I was released was to go to Khotso House to pay my respects to my bosses, the workers, who were very angry when they saw me because I had lost a lot of weight and really I was a different person altogether. It was good to be with them, and I encouraged the Edgars workers to continue with the action they were taking. It was for a good cause, and a very important strike in the sense that the workers were doing things themselves, which must have shown management that I was not the evil-doer they may have thought I was. Here were workers out on strike without anybody necessarily having 'instigated' it. The cause was low wages, but that strike was to lead to an agreement between CCAWUSA and Edgars.

Following that came the Woolworth's strike, in August, which began when one of the workers, Albert Rammova, didn't come into work one day and was dismissed. I'd been involved with Woolworth's before, but this time I came across several senior persons that I had not met.

The negotiations were held in Cape Town, but before we got there to sit round a table and work things out some of the senior executives, including the Personnel Director, Mr R.W. Stern, came to Khotso House, where the workers were gathered. I had told these executives what the workers had told me: that they would not go back unless Albert was reinstated, and that then it was to be without any strings attached – without loss of pay, without anything. But since these people thought I hadn't done enough, they were prepared to come and address the workers themselves, and so I said, 'Okay, I'll arrange that meeting. You come and speak to them here.'

And they came to Khotso House: tall, huge, bombastic, upright – bosses as they used to be. And we were almost 1,000 workers, packed into the hall. I remember so well the scene when the employers walked in and wanted to address us, and all those workers started singing a song, to say, 'Emma, we want to know what they want here,' and 'Emma, did you allow them to come and talk to us?' and so forth.

I said, 'Well, let's give them the opportunity. Let them talk to you.'

Well, the workers made their demands. And the employers said, 'If you don't go back to work you're dismissed.' And, 'You're fired – you're all *fired*,' and so forth. And the workers told them 'We're all fired as it is. You keep your jobs.'

So we had to negotiate further. I had a very active Chairman of the union at that time, Isaac Padi, and he also would come in, and we would sit across the night, bargaining with these employers, until we could go no further, and we had to go to Cape Town.

When we got there I met the Director of Woolworth's, Mr Susman, who said to me as I came in the room, 'Oh, my God, this person we fear so much. I thought she was a very big ogre of a person, yet it's just a tiny giant coming in.'

Well, he said he found I was someone he could talk to, and indeed we did have a good meeting, at the end of which the workers were reinstated and were also given the 50 rand increase they wanted.

But there was a lot to do there, at Woolworth's. Workers in Woolworth's had said they would never join the union because they thought that Woolworth's was the best company in South Africa, until our unions went in for this dismissal and we began to look at their conditions. And then, believe me, we found many faults.

There were no promotions for black people in the retail stores. You got the job and you stayed in it. And there were only selective wage increases, just for those the management wanted to reward. The wages were terrible. Very very bad. Women suffered from having to go on confinement leave, because you had to have completed two years with the company and to have a very good record as well, or you would not qualify. You never knew if you had that very good record. You would just hear from them that you did or didn't have it. It was like this with everything, management using its 'discretion' the whole time. So we worked to say there should be a structure based on more than management's prerogative.

Even when the workers went back the employers were not happy. I would receive phone calls from them complaining that when the workers walked in they did not say, 'Good morning, sir, good morning, Mr Joseph', and so forth. So I said, 'What did they say?' They told me the workers were saying, 'Good morning, comrade,' and they did not accept this as a form of address to them.

So now the comrade war started. I said, 'What does "comrade" mean? Is "Good morning, comrade" not the same as saying, "Good morning, colleague"?' Of course it was the Marxist association, and someone was saying only recently that 'comrade' was another word for youth now in South Africa. But to them I said, 'Well, you will just have to live with it or reject it. You either greet back or you don't. But the most important thing here is the workers are not assembled there for greetings. They are assembled for being productive at work. They are either productive or they are not productive. So they either greet and you greet them back, or you don't greet them back because you are offended by "comrade".'

Another thing which offended them was that some of the workers when they walked past, instead of saying 'Good morning' at all, said '*Amandla*', which means power, and which has a reply, 'The power is ours.' This was driving them crazy, because they knew that immediately the workers withdrew their power from work that whole place would again be at a standstill. What with this and the comrade war we had phone calls and phone calls, from the most senior industrial relations personnel in Cape Town. But it died down, and we could go on with our real purpose there, which was to use our recognition and carry on with the improvement of working conditions and wages, and have unfair labour practices done away with.

Also in August was the strike at OK Bazaars. Here the starting point was wages again, and this was another long and arduous strike. The feelings of the workers in this country are so strong. They put up with so much, and when they turn around and say they have had enough, my God, they do mean it. So they have it in their hearts and minds that something must happen, and you are caught up in their determination and their fight, but at the same time you have to direct this anger into a constructive dialogue with another very angry group of people, the employers, and this takes all your strength. Once we even had to step in to protect one of the management, who was found spying in a meeting at Khotso House during the second week of that strike, and was punched and kicked by the workers, and even hit on the head by some women, with their shoes, until one of our officials stepped in and rescued him!

But again we won, and again we managed to sign an agreement with the employers. And in October, with these three battles behind us, we had the last of that year's big strikes, at the Central News Agency (CNA).[1] Here a meeting we had arranged with the management to discuss pay and recognition was cancelled when they turned down our request to have three CNA workers accompany the CCAWUSA officials. The following week about 600 workers went on strike, and they were followed by more. This dispute was resolved in just over a week, a week of hard talking and long meetings with the workers, who never wanted just to sit at home if they were on strike but would come into Khotso House and cram themselves into the hall there, because they wanted to be together, and they knew that their solidarity and togetherness were their most powerful weapon. But that was a very long week for me, with that wonderful but demanding union presence at Khotso House and those long, long meetings with management – the last one, I remember, lasted seven and a half hours.

So by the end of that year we had won these four big battles, and with these recognitions we really had in our hands the power to change things. In reaction to this, from their fear of us, the management did all they could to discredit CCAWUSA. In 1983 a magazine called *Hard Labour*, edited by Gavin Brown, a legal

---

[1] CNA is a large distribution chain operating throughout South Africa, distributing newspapers, magazines and books.

adviser to OK Bazaars, produced a pamphlet discrediting CCAWUSA that had been widely distributed in shopping centres, parking lots and warehouses. In it were questions like: Who is controlling CCAWUSA? Where does the subscription money go? And so on. It was 'signed' by the Edgars shop stewards, but at a meeting of the Edgars shop stewards shortly after they all said the pamphlet was not their work. I am glad to say that our members were not so easily fooled!

But for myself, what with the tension and the exhaustion, I must say that I was beginning to feel the strain, and to realise that I was not so quickly to recover from my experience as a detainee.

Because through all this I just could not forget the prison. This came to a head when Alan Fine, who was still detained, wanted me to go and visit him. I wanted to, but I hated the thought of going to that place. To go back to prison after you've come out is really horrible.

But I did go to visit him. I walked through those gates, and I could hear every gate being locked behind me, and as I listened to all those closing doors I wasn't thinking about Alan. I was just thinking, Will this door open for me to go out again?

There was no contact allowed between Alan and me. I could touch Tom when he came to see me, and speak to him and so forth, but with Alan there was glass dividing us. Still, he was very pleased to see me, and I was pleased to see him, even with all that glass dividing us.

By now he was charged. They were saying he had been communicating with SACTU through dead letter boxes, and that this constituted terrorism and was furthering the aims of the ANC. And this exposed the ignorance, or contempt, of the South African government for the laws they themselves had made, because SACTU was not a banned organisation, and when this was brought up in his trial by the defence they had to agree he had done nothing illegal. But that was after more than a year – a wasted year of his life. He was also accused of communicating with Jeanette Curtis, who was in exile in Botswana then, but Alan Fine and Jeanette were old friends, and he was her eldest daughter's godfather, and whatever they were communicating about was ordinary business.[1]

---

[1] Jeanette Curtis went into exile in 1977 and worked for SACTU. She was killed by a letter-bomb in Angola in 1984. It is widely believed that the bomb was the work of South African agents.

But there, in that prison room, we were only able to have general conversation. He wanted to know what things were like, and so forth, and how was the union, and he asked me to give his regards here and there. And afterwards I was pleased I had gone to see him, but I could not do it a second time.

The other thing I had to do was visit Neil Aggett's grave. I called Liz Floyd, Neil's girlfriend, to ask her to take me there. She had come out of prison in February, but she said to me, 'Emma, I don't know it. I've never been there.'

I said, 'It's my tradition. He was dear and close to me. I must go to his grave.' And I made this arrangement with Liz. We went to a friend, who gave us some plants, and we took hand forks and so forth, and we went to the cemetery. A woman friend who had attended the funeral accompanied us, and we looked for Neil's grave. When we found it we saw a wreath on top, on which was written that a Communist was buried in this grave.

Well, we told ourselves it didn't come from the people. We just left it there. We had heard that already there was a lot of vandalism with the grave. Many people knew where it was, because Neil had a big cathedral service, with many speakers, and his funeral was indeed a funeral of the people.

By the grave I said a prayer. I said a prayer and told Neil how much I cared for him, how much I loved him. Here we were two women together: myself, a black woman, and Liz Floyd, a white woman I've always respected and honoured. But with this friend we shared, this dead friend, we became as one.

This has continued. We are friends. She has been affected the same as all of us. I remember when my problems were continuing and I was suffering from high blood pressure, I went to Liz Floyd as a doctor and asked her to treat me. But when I went and told her about all my problems it was like a psychological release. I started emptying and talking, and it was a great relief. This was not a doctor and patient discussing. It was two friends who'd come from prison, and prison is not something you can leave behind.

Those six months brought about a great change in me. I tried to get it all out at the time, all the bad feelings and memories, but I could not, and even now there are things that come up, and I remember. These are long-term effects. I have had long-term physical effects, and long-term mental effects.

The first time I had caught sight of myself in a mirror after all that time I had been shocked. I was a different person altogether. I am a very big person by stature, a fat person, though not tall. But now I was so thin and small, and my complexion had gone so fair from being in the shade for all that time, that I couldn't believe my eyes that this was me. It shook me a lot. I thought it was my sister in that bathroom with me, my sister who is very fair.

After the loss of my teeth, caused by the terrible food I was given in Pretoria, I had to be fitted for dentures when I was in Denmark. And I have to put something on my nails to patch them, because they are always splitting and they hurt. And I have a problem with my bladder, from sitting flat on concrete floors for all that time. I'd never had these problems before, not like most women. I've always been a person who was troubled with tonsils, but never with gyny problems. But now I was advised to have a hysterectomy, much earlier than I should have had it because I was suffering with fibroids.

I was admitted to the Johannesburg General Hospital, which was originally a hospital only for whites. But the white community built a very modern, up-to-date hospital for their community and turned over their rundown hospital to black patients. The whites-only hospital which dominates the horizon of Johannesburg stands as a symbol of the attitude of whites to their own health-care and welfare: for their comparatively small community they have built an enormous hospital; our infinitely larger community has inherited their rejects.

On my day of admission a young male white doctor came to my bedside and a tray with instruments was brought. He was joined by another white doctor, an elderly man. They stood on either side of my bed and the young doctor started examining my vagina and seemed to be demonstrating something to the elderly doctor, who was taking notes. While the young doctor was inserting something into me they were talking. Then the elderly doctor left and the young doctor was joined by another white male doctor. The young doctor was now relating what he had previously done to me in the first examination and I realised that he was being examined by a professor. I was inwardly fuming, and when they had finished and were about to move away I said to them that I regretted that their bedside manner was so horrible. I asked why they never informed me that I was going to be used as a guinea pig for their exams. I added that I had been humanely examined by a gynaecologist the previous year in Denmark, where I was treated as a human being. I said that they had also failed to prepare me for what they were going to do – that the speculum would feel cold and that it would hurt as they inserted it. They answered defensively, saying they did not know that I could speak English, but neither was at all apologetic.

While I was there in that hospital I received a letter from Inge Genefke which meant very much to me. She was thanking me for a gift I had sent her. She wrote:

My dearest Emma,
Before my eyes is the beautiful blue box with hearts in every corner, and inside the violet heart which I have not touched. Before my eyes is also the beautiful flower card, where you have promised me to be selfish, as I asked you to be.

In my ears is your voice, and I am very unhappy, because I feel that you are not at all selfish, you are not at all taking care of yourself. You know, we are all here your friends for life, and we are very worried about you.

We do not understand why you have been operated on, Emma. Professor John Philip will write you with good advice as to what you have to do and not to do after an operation. May I add that after such an operation, you will be tired and depressive for about half a year at least. You have to take it very easy during that year and not work too much, please.

We have followed you in our thoughts. We still do, and we will always do; but recently I have started getting nightmares because of fear for you, Emma. You are so precious for everyone. You should lead a life for the moment – say for about 4–6 months – without working very much. I know this will be very difficult for you, but it is so important in order to enable you to work for a long time afterwards . . .

For your family, Tom and your daughters, I do hope everything is okay.

Dear Emma, take care, very much care of yourself. I send you my love, and you know that whatever we can do which might help you – even a little bit – we will all do so.

Love
Inge

Two other bad things were the exhaustion and the loss of memory. When I went back to work that first time, in August, I was almost like a cabbage. I, who had always been a very productive person, now had to struggle to keep going. For a long time I felt like this. I felt that although I was free, I was still a condemned person.

It still meant so much to me to see my youngest daughter, Dudu. It meant so much, and then I heard from her that Bishop Tutu had made an arrangement for her to come and see me in January. He didn't tell me he had done this, but when I heard I was so happy. On Christmas Day, I remember, I went to the church where Bishop Tutu was preaching, and I thanked him for what he had done.

Coming back from the church, I felt exhausted, from the heat and everything, and when I got home I went to bed. I spent the whole of Christmas Day sleeping, and then Boxing Day as well. On 27 December my husband said he was driving into town. He said later he wasn't aware that I wasn't myself. He told me I said I was coming to town with him, and he said his car was giving him trouble. I said, 'Well, I can take a taxi or bus to go to hospital.' He said I insisted I wanted to go to hospital.

We drove together, and the car broke down somewhere in the outskirts of the city. He said he left me in the car and that he told me he was coming back. Then he went to get somebody to tow him, and when he came back and didn't find me in the car he thought I'd taken a taxi and proceeded to hospital.

I don't remember anything of what happened. I just remember feeling vaguely that I was walking back to Soweto. I know I went to a service station, and I stopped there and asked, 'How do I walk back to Soweto?' And they gave me the directions. I remember that. 'Walk that way, walk that way.' And I was walking, walking.

I must have got tired along the way, and I sat somewhere on the sidewalk. I was very tired and I didn't know what was going on. It happened that Tom's first cousin was driving into town, and he says he saw a person and noticed it was me. He did a U-turn and found me sitting there, and as he spoke to me he could see I was not right in my mind, and he took me into his car.

He drove me straight back to Soweto. There was no one at home, so they took me to my brother's house in Dube. My brother's wife and my brother then packed me into the car and took me to our family doctor, Dr Nathatho Motlana. I don't remember any of this. It is just what I have been told. Dr Motlana told them I was very unwell, and they took me back to their home and started looking for Tom.

When they found Tom and told him, he was surprised. He reported what had happened to the DPSC, and they said I must be taken to hospital. They recommended me to go to Professor Koornhof, who is the brother of Piet Koornhof, but a very different kind of person.[1] Professor Koornhof wrote a letter to another doctor, who had to examine me, and I was then admitted to Johannesburg Hospital.

I was treated with drugs, and I spent most of the time from after Christmas until somewhere around the middle of January sleeping. But as well as the drugs they gave me a similar treatment to Inge's. They said I had still not spoken out, and I was still very much in need of that kind of therapy.

The trouble was, I knew that Dudu was about to come, and I didn't want her to find me in hospital, so when the doctors insisted that I should remain in hospital I refused. I wanted her to find me at home. It was important to me that Dudu should not know that I had, as it was, lost my senses.

I was very pleased that the day she came home she found me there, and that I was myself, a strong person. I was okay. And the week that she spent with me – it was only for a week, she had to rush to go back – was the best of times I've ever had, and I was so grateful to Desmond Tutu for arranging this for me.

I was to suffer more memory lapses, though. They came at a certain time of year, particularly in December. The first thing that I would experience was a feeling of tiredness, exhaustion, and then I would go into a deep sleep. And thereafter I never knew what happened.

One Sunday in the December of 1983 I went out to Tom, who was in the garden, and said I was going to have a rest. I went to bed. I still don't know what happened next, but when I came round on

[1] Piet Koornhof was at that time South Africa's Minister of Co-operation and Development. Professor H. J. Koornhof became involved in the DPSC when his daughter Hannchen was in detention. She was charged, in April-May 1982, under the Internal Security Act with passing on a code which could be used to communicate with ANC members in Botswana. She had already been held for seven months as a Terrorism Act detainee.

Monday morning there was blood all over the floor and I found I had lost the nail of my big toe and that I had swellings here and there on my body. Tom says the next thing he saw was me walking out of the house, nearly naked. I don't remember that. We looked around for my toenail, thinking maybe if we found it it would provide a clue as to how I got in that mess, but we couldn't find it anywhere.

I had nightmares, too. When I first came out every car move shattered me. And the thought of going back – well, when they say one gets cold feet I really know what that means. It's not just a saying. Sometimes, even in great heat, when I am perspiring and so forth, my feet are so frozen I have to cover them up.

I did manage to break my memory lapses, at least. In December 1985 my husband and family suggested I leave South Africa to see if I still suffered a lapse. So I went to Dudu, and indeed it never did come. I try always to travel at this time of year now.

For a long time I didn't talk to my family about my prison experiences. Neither Dudu nor Molly knew about many of the things I had been through until they saw me in *Mama, I'm Crying,* telling of the terrible time I could not remember Dudu's name. They kept saying, 'Mom, you never told us about this.' They didn't even know about my forgetting Dudu's name. This book will serve as a living memory of the evil of the apartheid regime. It is an opportunity for me to speak to my children.

Perhaps the effects of my detention would not be so unpleasant if I was not constantly bothered by the security forces. But since I have been out of prison, practically every eve of every black commemoration day – like 16 June (Soweto Massacre), 26 June (Freedom Charter), 21 March (Sharpeville Day) – I have been reminded of these dates by the shining torches and loud knocks at my door which mean I am once again being visited by the security branch. They search my home as though I am harbouring people who are their targets.

On one such visit there was a young girl in the back room who was staying with us while she studied for her exams. There was a loud knock on our front door. We hastened to open it, because we did not want it to be kicked in. Two young security men greeted us politely, saying they wanted to search our house. With the State of Emergency they do not even require search warrants. All we could do was ask why they needed to search our home. They said, very politely, that it was routine.

As we let them in we heard our young student in the back room screaming with terror, because at the same time as these polite young men were entering at the front, more security men had scaled our back wall and were kicking open the door of the girl's room. Tom and I protested fiercely at their double standards of politeness at the front door while secretly attacking from the back of the house.

They searched under the beds, in cupboards, in toilets and in the dustbins, and having found nothing were prepared to leave. We insisted that the men who scaled our back wall should not go through our front door but must return the way they came.

Once, in November 1988, two white security men came to my home and questioned me about my travelling abroad, and whether I was going to Lusaka to get a mandate from my president, Oliver Tambo. I responded that the president of both CCAWUSA and the Anglican Church were in South Africa, and I had no need to travel abroad to meet them.

And only recently, in February 1988, I was summoned to report to Protea police station, just outside Soweto. When I received this summons I just thought of the months I had spent in solitary confinement, and I got so scared that I requested my lawyer, David Dyson, to accompany me. I did not know whether I would be free to return to my home after questioning. This request was refused by the police, so some of my close friends, Leah Tutu, Joyce Seroke, who is General Secretary of the YWCA, Nonia Rampomane and my daughter Molly, accompanied me to Protea, to give me support.

On that visit I was quite terrified. We went through the security gate and up to the front entrance, where I pressed the buzzer. A disembodied voice asked me what I wanted, and I responded that I had an appointment with a security officer. The response of this anonymous voice quite frightened me. He asked, 'Why are the other people with you?' I realised then that we were being observed by a hidden camera. I replied that they were my friends accompanying me. After some time the voice told me that the security officer was not in.

My friends returned to their work, and I also returned to work, feeling very angry that my day had been disrupted for no good reason. I determined not to return to Protea.

The same afternoon I received a phone call from the security officer that I must return to Protea the next day. I verified this with my lawyer, who suggested that for my own well-being and because of the State of Emergency I should comply with their request.

Molly, Leah and Joyce accompanied me once again, and I was filled with anguish when this time they were turned away even at the first security gate. I had to proceed alone. I wondered what was going to become of me.

The security man was dressed neatly in civilian clothes and greeted me very warmly. He rose from the chair and asked me to sit down. The politer he was, the more frightened I felt. I had suffered at the merciless hands of 'kind' white interrogators. Also present at this meeting was a black security man, who had escorted me to the office. The first thing I noticed when I entered the room was that the walls were decorated with the names and information of all the trade unions.

The opening question to me was, 'Did you have to go around the world telling everyone that I had asked to see you? Why did you tell your lawyer? What harm did you expect from me? I am here to help you.' I responded by saying, 'In what way can you help us when your security people are the cause of our problems?' (This was at the height of the school boycotts, and the children were continuously harassed by security.) He responded that our children were undisciplined. As he said this all my fright evaporated, and I even forgot where I was as I replied and told him about the inferior education which was handed down to our children.

He asked me why I considered the education inferior. I told him that even though I had to leave school before completing Junior Certificate I still had received a superior education under the Transvaal Education Department, as opposed to Bantu Education, which was initiated by the Nationalist government in the 1950s. What pleased me as I spoke was to see the young black security man nodding his head in agreement as I made my points.

Finally he raised the question of my travels abroad and meeting with the ANC. I was reminded once again how far-reaching are the tentacles of the Special Branch. He said, 'You travel the whole world and don't have a pleasant word to say about South Africa but I notice you keep returning to this country. Haven't you managed to find a better country to live in?'

I said I was born here and that it was my country and I intended to stay here. On leaving he asked if he could see me again and I responded that I saw no necessity for a further meeting.

I cannot possibly write of every incident like these ones, but one in particular stays in my mind because my children were affected. It was in late 1987, and Nomsa, my youngest daughter, who was 24 at the time, was taking a stroll three streets away from our house, with her boyfriend Jabu. She saw many security police and soldiers parking cars and getting out and taking their caps off so that they would not so easily be identified. The minute Nomsa saw them she and Jabu decided to run home because they felt they were making for our house. So they returned a few minutes before the invasion and we were prepared for their onslaught. Once again everyone was questioned, including Nomsa and Jabu, and the house was thoroughly searched.

So it is not only Tom and myself that suffer but also our gentle daughter Nomsa who is upset by these searches.

Some time around February 1983 I went back to work again, but my concentration was still very bad, and again I was recommended not to work full-time. I tried this, but again it was impossible. You can't cut yourself completely off from doing the type of work we were involved in. If I stayed at home and didn't go to the office I would take my work home with me. And when I couldn't concentrate and suffered from forgetfulness I said to myself, I think I've got to continue having treatment. But I didn't want to go to hospital again. It reminded me of too many things. A friend recommended that I should see a private psychotherapist, but said it would cost me. I said, 'I am prepared to spend for my health.'

Psychotherapy for us Africans is something very new. I never thought before that a normal person, not suffering from anything, would go for psychiatric treatment. But now I want to recommend it to many people. I read a notice on the wall of the place I went to which said, 'PSYCHIATRIC TREATMENT IS A BREATHER FOR THE MIND.' I wanted to go and say that to everyone, because although I went there as a patient, thereafter I really began to think that many people would benefit from treatment. With all the stresses and strains we go through, there's a great need for therapy of this kind.

But then there is the taboo, the stigma. If you walk into that building, which is in the city centre, in Bree Street, then everybody knows it's for your mental health and thinks, 'What is wrong?' And the other thing is that most of the doctors who are trained to be psychotherapists are white, and it would take black people much time to get used to it, and to unwind, although most of the people who have been in detention now do go for psychotherapy, which is good.

I once discussed this with a lecturer at a graduate business school. I said, 'May we for once concentrate on the minds, because once we have the minds we are really beginning to make an investment in South Africa. Let us think about things which are there to stay in South Africa. Let us think about a better society.' And if our children can really think about this kind of training – training to provide a breather for the mind – it would do that. It would help to produce a better society.

12

Violent Times

When I started CCAWUSA I can remember I told myself I would give it ten years and then it would be time to move. Well, after ten years, in May 1985, I announced I would leave the following year, and I did. I felt it was time to go, and not once since have I looked back with regret that I left at that time. To have gone before, when I came out of detention, would have been to tell the government that they had won. And to have stayed for longer would have been to wear out my strength and my energy. I felt I had seen CCAWUSA through its opening chapters, from being a union with no members to being a union with over 80,000, with power and influence and with great achievements behind it.

The main thing that the union brought to light was the number of unfair dismissals in the commercial sector. The wages were so terribly low, and employers could just drive workers the way they wanted. And the workers were so terribly suppressed. Even with the very little knowledge they had about their rights they could not speak out, because in South Africa once a white employer says, 'You're cheeky,' then that is that. You never know what is meant by cheeky. You speak back, you are cheeky. You don't speak back, you are cheeky. But no one will actually define or give you an analysis of what cheeky is – and indeed that would be hard, when you reflect on the abusive language and swear-words that management feel are an acceptable means of communication with their workers.

The working conditions of black workers were frequently lacking in any concern for their health. I found myself again and again shocked at their treatment, particularly of women. I heard of expectant mothers who were forced to work in refrigeration rooms, and one of the practices we came across that still fills me with a sense of outrage was the searching of black women workers in some of the stores and workplaces, where white women were empowered to make black women employees strip naked, even if they were menstruating. They were forced to remove their sanitary towels, and most of the searching was highly personal and very embarrassing. They would examine even the vagina and the anal area.

In 1983, at PEP Stores, a national department store with its headquarters in Cape Town, one of the branches in Vereeniging, Transvaal, was the centre of protest. Six black women refused to be stripped naked by the manageress and they were dismissed from work. This unfair dismissal came to the Vereeniging branch of CCAWUSA, and was brought to the attention of the head office.

We had a meeting to decide how best to hit at this matter, and decided, because of the numerous complaints we had received regarding searching throughout the country, to expose PEP stores by phoning the press. We said we regarded body searching as degrading to anybody, but that we felt even more angry that only black women were subjected to it.

This story hit the headlines, and as a result of the bad publicity the PEP head office contacted me from Cape Town and arranged a meeting which took place in my CCAWUSA offices, in Khotso House.

While waiting for that meeting, CCAWUSA organised a protest outside the PEP store in Vereeniging. Black men and black women were very angry during this protest, and we had many phone calls of support, some even from other managements, saying how disgusting it was.

Our meeting with the PEP management was on 19 May 1983. We called the six workers who were dismissed to give evidence, and they came in one by one. In their anger they were not prepared to give only a verbal statement, but physically showed what had been done to them. It was not at my instigation that the women insisted on lifting their skirts to show what they had been subjected to, but I was very proud and pleased that they did. The management, on the other hand – all those male executives from Cape Town – could not tolerate it. They said it was humiliating and disgusting, and the women were forced to stop. All six women were reinstated that day, and were fully paid for the whole time since their dismissal. There was an agreement between the union and management that they should stop searching workers and should work out an acceptable policy of store security. I could not help reflecting on the irony of this body searching of poor black women workers in the light of the corruption of those whites in high government office who have been exposed in the last few years. Minister after minister has resigned for expropriating millions of rands and salting the money away in numbered bank accounts around the world.

When a union has proper recognition agreements, the employers must agree to grievance procedures, so that the workers cannot be dismissed right, left and centre at management's discretion. Even before those agreements, though, I must say people were always puzzled to discover the strength of workers' feelings on this matter. Unfair dismissals started many of the strikes during my years in the union. The dismissal of one worker could result in hundreds of workers going out on strike, even though shopworkers do not have a focus like a factory, where you can stop work and bring the entire machinery to a standstill.

It remains one of my prides that part of the agreement we made covering OK Bazaars established for the first time the right of confinement leave with a guarantee of return afterwards, either to the position the worker had left or to a similar position. And if they were to be changed from one store to another, that must be negotiated with the worker, and agreed. In that deal we also fought to have women included in medical aid and pension funds, which had previously been only for men. And together with that I would add to the main achievements of our union the increases in wages which we were always struggling for. Because of course it is always the black workers who are earning the least, and mainly the black woman workers. The money is important, and we should never forget that, much as we might be fighting injustices and claiming human rights for each and every black person. The money must always be seen as part of that injustice, and that right. Equality is important, and the money stands for that.

One of the strikes that delighted me in our divided land was the CCAWUSA strike at the Checkers supermarket in Germiston, in 1983. This was unique in that black women were striking for a white woman who had been demoted. She was not even a member of CCAWUSA, so they should not constitutionally have come out for her, but it was wonderful for me to see this expression of support across the colour bar, and the victory these workers won heartens me for a post-apartheid South Africa.

No country that lives by a system of apartheid can claim a sense of justice for itself, not in the area of black and white relations, and not in the area of relations between men and women either, whether white or black. The segregation, the setting of one off against another – this breeds a corruption from which none of us, whatever our colour, can be free. This was brought home to me when I left CCAWUSA, and I wanted so very much for my position to be filled by a woman. It would have made me so happy to see a woman ready there, wanting to do that job, and prepared to jostle the men around her for it. I had had a bitter experience in the time when COSATU came to be formed, when I had taken such a lot of interest, and worked so hard, and had seen how all the men were very happy to consult with me because of the size and importance of my union. It didn't matter then that I was a woman. But then came the day when the names were put forward of those who would go on the National Executive. And each and every one of those names were men's names. Even CCAWUSA was represented in the end not by me, who was its General Secretary, but by Makhulu Ledwaba, who was the President, even though he was a much younger person, and was to be the youngest of all the people on the executive. And most ironic of all, when they were having an important person to come and meet them, from abroad or whatever, then they would say, 'Oh, Emma, please, you must meet them.' And I would say, 'Am I again just to be used as a valve, just to patch up what you have done wrong?'

There was in fact worse to come, because the next step was to choose a logo for COSATU. And all the logos that came about, every single one, had the image of a man. There was not a single image of a woman. So it means that our presence – our efforts, our work, our support – was not even recognised. And CCAWUSA, which is regarded as a very strong woman-orientated group fighting for women's rights, with a majority, 60 per cent, of women as members, had to speak up for the very rights we had fought for from the different employers.

All this must be the concern of the union movement. The trade union movement is a very powerful organisation, and it is not there just to look at the bread and butter problems of workers. The trade union movement is concerned with the liberation of the people in South Africa. Because if the trade union organisation cannot take on the issue of the liberation of the country, who will? Much as they have abolished the pass laws, who wants to be a member of the Nationalist Party? Who wants to be a member of the PFP? No black wants to be a member of these organisations. There have been two organisations for my people and they have been banned. These are the Pan-African Congress, the ANC, and now the UDF. So the government has got to unban these organisations, and allow the people the choice of saying which political organisation they want to belong to. But until then, in the absence of these organisations, the trade unions are the people who must fight their battles. The trade unions have got to follow the workers in all their travels – to get them home, and to school, in the education and welfare of their children, everywhere. The whole life of a worker needs trade union involvement. And together with that goes the whole question of equality between men and women.

One of the most important victories for the trade union movement, and one which for me closed a chapter that had opened when I first tried to meet with management as a trade union leader, was in 1986, when I came up against my old friend Ray Ackerman, of Pick 'n' Pay. We in South Africa were appealing to trade unionists in Australia to stop the expansion of Pick 'n' Pay in their country. We regarded the move to develop in Australia as grossly unfair. I myself had had many disputes with Pick 'n' Pay, over a number of years, concerning their exploitation of black workers. I now felt strongly that it was on the strength of the profits of this exploitation that they were opening new markets in Australia. It angered me that these multinational companies, instead of using their wealth to bring an end to apartheid, were instead benefiting from it, and at the same time cushioning themselves against the eventuality of black liberation and the fairer distribution of the wealth of the country. They are building up fortunes outside of South Africa so that come what may they can continue their luxuries and comforts elsewhere.

I was elated when the Australian trade unions showed solidarity with our cause, and was thrilled to read in the London *Financial Times*, on 20 February 1986, that 'industrial action by an Australian union [the Plumbers' and Gasfitters' Union] has compelled Pick 'n' Pay to abandon plans to build a hypermarket in Melbourne'.

Once again the Australian trade unions had risen to the challenge, and had demonstrated their solidarity that an injury to one is an injury to all. It reminded me again that in April 1982, after the DPSC had battled that those of us who were imprisoned without charge or trial, and in solitary confinement, should be allowed to have transistor radios, Tom had brought one to me and I had been able to hear of Neil Aggett's 'suicide', and that trade unions in Australia were refusing to unload South African goods in protest.

That March I was invited, as a trade unionist and also as a member of Women Against Apartheid, to a meeting with the Commonwealth Eminent Persons Group (EPG). This group consisted of distinguished leaders of the Commonwealth, and had been allowed into South Africa as a fact-finding team. They were granted access to all the political forces in South Africa, and were even allowed to visit Nelson Mandela.

I was very pleased to be at that meeting, because I wanted to challenge Malcolm Fraser, ex-Prime Minister of Australia and Co-Chairman of the Group, regarding South African multinationals opening in his country. I reminded him that while trade unionists had prevented Pick 'n' Pay from opening in Melbourne, Pick 'n' Pay still had a branch in Brisbane, which had opened the previous year, and that when the Brisbane branch opened the prices were so competitive that there was a stampede and one person died as a result. I pointed out that the reason they could price themselves so low was simply that the exploitation of their black workers in South Africa enhanced their profits. Mr Fraser listened attentively to my comments, which were supported by the general meeting.

The findings of the EPG were published in 1986. They have not been acted upon by the South African government.

You can never relax in this country, this South Africa. With each step forward comes a step backwards. They gave the black unions the right to register, and then they swooped on the leaders and arrested those in the forefront of the black trade union movement. And now, with the stronger position of black unions and improving industrial relations, they are bringing in a new plan, which they are calling Racial Mix.

Before I left CCAWUSA I one day received information pushed

under my door, at my office and at home, about this Racial Mix.
Workers are very good characters. They will gather information, and
even when they don't want you to know who actually delivered it
they will get it to you. So here was a circular letter with the heading
'Racial Mix'. It said that from now on, henceforth, every black worker
should be replaced with a worker of another race. You must mix the
races on the shop floor, because during work stoppages the blacks
are the ones that support stoppages most. Therefore, never replace a
black with a black. They didn't necessarily say, 'Replace them with a
Coloured, Indian or white,' and this was deliberate, because when
you speak with people who do not have all the information you find
that 'Racial Mix' is seen as a symptom of development in South
Africa.

Another new policy is the introduction of new legislation
involving extended trading hours. Here again they are giving
themselves excuses to say, 'We cannot employ black people who
will have to be coming from Soweto for these late or difficult hours,
because it is not easy to convey them from their homes.' So they
will again be developing their plan of Racial Mix, and justifying
themselves in their selective choosing of workers.

Similarly with the talk about shareholding. Ray Ackerman of Pick
'n' Pay is one of those offering this scheme, and we are supposed to
be so pleased to be offered shares in his company. But I was told,
'Never accept a cup of tea' because it is capitalist versus worker, and
the worker is not equal. So I say, 'Only once we are equal and are
trained and participating in the Stock Exchange so that we can
examine our dividends – only when we are in a position to
understand for ourselves whether there is profit or no profit – and
only when we are paid more than breadline wages and have a
surplus – only then will we decide to invest, and then *we* will be the
ones to decide how.'

As we make strides towards further change, this government is
also making preparations to counter our every move. Take, for
example, the bombing of COSATU House, in May of 1987. To destroy
that building – the building I was involved in finding, that was our
centre as workers – well, whoever did that deed made sure that that
building was utterly destroyed, and that trade unions were
fragmented all over again in their efforts to find a place in which to
gather. And then, towards the end of August 1988, I attended a board

meeting in Namibia on behalf of the Department of Justice and Reconciliation. We had spent three days in the north, which is the war zone, and on our return to Windhoek we learnt that a massive bomb explosion had devastated Khotso House. The explosion took place on 31 August at 1.03 am, and damage to the building was estimated at 1 million rand. Fortunately no one was hurt, although all the workers who were asleep on the sixth floor were severely shocked. Before leaving for Namibia I had asked a colleague to park my car in the underground garage of Khotso, for 'safety'. Now, on the TV news, I saw my car mashed under the rubble of the building.

As soon as the board received the news of this attack it was decided that we would go and pray in one of the parishes in Windhoek. On our way back to the conference centre after the service we witnessed a building blown up in front of our eyes, and as a result of that bomb blast two people were killed, and others injured. We are thankful to God that no one was hurt in Khotso House.

A few months after Khotso House was bombed, the Catholic church in Pretoria was burnt down. In South Africa, when the darkest forces of evil arraign themselves in this way against the work of God, the culprits are never found or arrested. There is no place for neutrality in this crisis we find ourselves in. We are all too aware that these blasts take place in an atmosphere of hatred, which is generated against all organisations and church bodies opposed to apartheid. We are forced to join the growing squatter community in their pain of having nowhere to stay, and we know full well that in this country, where black people are treated as less than human, the question of human rights and dignity can never arise.

The police have now made an announcement that the bomb was put into Khotso House by the people who work there, and that it inadvertently went off before being used on its intended target. They claim to be looking for several ANC members. The Church has protested strongly at the suggestion that they might be involved in bombings.

Sadly, as black determination to be free increases, so does the virulent right wing grow in number. Their fear and greed increases their hatred. The numerous right-wing organisations in South Africa may differ on certain issues of policy, strategy and tactics, but one idea is common to them all: they identify blacks as the enemy. The grotesque slaughter in Pretoria in 1988 epitomises the right wing. Mr Strydom, a member of the Afrikaner Weerstand Beweging (AWB), simply woke up one morning and with his sawn-off shotgun went on a hunting expedition. He killed seven innocent black people and wounded many others. He is a man in his twenties. He has been declared sane and will stand trial. He smiles and waves to his family and friends in the courtroom and looks distinctly proud of his achievement on behalf of the Boere Volk (Boer Nation). One lives in a constant state of fear of these people. They cannot be under-estimated, and as their numbers grow they remain a very real and dangerous threat to black people, and even to those white people who stand up to be counted with us in the struggle and are labelled by their right-wing white brethren as Communists and Kaffir-boeties (black brothers).

This is the kind of violence which surrounds the apartheid regime. This is the kind of society we live in – a society where children disappear, where mothers go from prison to prison to try and find their children, where some of those picked up by the troops or the police are as young as eleven years old. And in this kind of society it is not difficult to fan hatred, mistrust and revenge. The authorities have skilfully manipulated black people, creating ethnic divisions by encouraging malicious rumours, and turning black against black rather than against their real enemy, which is apartheid. The horror of South Africa is that the life of a black person is very cheap. Under this brutal regime, the saddest turn of all is that some of our own people have become brutalised and a prey to violent feelings.

This has hit me personally very recently, when as a result of a long and unsubstantiated article in the *Sowetan* five undertakers were killed in different parts of Soweto on Friday, 4 March 1988. One of them was my dear son-in-law, Aubrey, the husband to my daughter Molly, father of her children.

Aubrey's death took place in Mshenguville, in Molofo, one of the most squalid and overcrowded of the squatter camps which have mushroomed in the ghetto of Soweto in the last two years. Hundreds and hundreds of homeless people have constructed tin shacks in which to live, in conditions in which it is hard to keep up human dignity. The government provides houses for the 'upwardly mobile' black middle class who can afford to pay their prices, but the homeless and the unemployed are left to rot. In such an area of despair, paranoia and hatred can easily be inflamed.

Aubrey was thirty-seven when he was killed. He had returned to South Africa in 1987 after studying in West Germany for the previous six years. He had obtained his BSc degree in agriculture at Fort Hare in South Africa and was then granted an Anglican Church scholarship to complete his Master's degree in Agriculture at the Technical University of Berlin. Molly and Aubrey had a very loving and close relationship, and it was made even closer by those many years living in a foreign country, far from their home.

They returned to their country, with their two children, Mphoentle (Beautiful Gift), aged thirteen, and Rirandzu (Love), aged eight, all speaking fluent German and with great excitement, with high hopes for their future. My grandchildren are very clever, and they can speak German so well that they have found a way to express their disapproval of me in that language, which I cannot understand. The other day, while sharing a meal, they said to their mother in German, 'You always told us not to talk with food in our mouths, so why is Gogo (Gran) doing that now?'

Aubrey had applied for a lectureship at a university, and while waiting for an interview he was helping his family in their undertaking business. In February 1988 the *Sowetan* published articles claiming that a terror gang driving an ambulance was abducting children in the townships, and then that as well as an ambulance there was a hearse, and that the abductors of innocent children were undertakers.

On that terrible Friday, 4 March 1988, Molly was driving home from work, having collected the children from school. She was driving past Mshenguville when she saw large crowds and billowing smoke. In the confusion of the crowd she suddenly spotted Aubrey, who approached her car and asked her to return home immediately and phone the police to come quickly because there was violence in that area. He said the man who was being assaulted was the driver, Alson Twala, an elderly man who had worked for Aubrey's parents for many years, and that the black smoke ahead of them was the burning hearse. Molly asked Aubrey where he was going, and he explained that he was going to plead with the assailants. He reassured Molly that he would be returning home in a short while.

Molly and the children returned home, which was less than five minutes' drive, and phoned Jabulani police station, who said that Mshenguville was not their area geographically. She phoned another police station, in Moroka, but they also failed to respond. Molly finally drove to the police station and pleaded with the police to come. Finally they agreed. By now the crowds had grown bigger, but still Aubrey had not returned home. As Molly pursued her way through the crowds to look for him, neighbours were stopping her from going closer to the burning hearse. The neighbours already knew that Aubrey was dead, and they did not wish Molly to see his burnt-out body.

Molly returned home and called me to say that she was anxious about her husband, who had still not returned. Nomsa and myself immediately drove to Molly's house. The neighbours were gathered outside, and they asked me not to leave Molly and the children there, but to take them back to my house. As we were driving off, one neighbour approached the car and whispered to me that my son-in-law was dead. With the shock, I gave it a deaf ear, and said nothing to Molly, but drove home.

At home I immediately phoned Roger, Molly's father, and told him that he must go in search of Aubrey. I still could not accept that he was dead. I then phoned the Mageza family and Aubrey's mother came to my house. Aubrey's family and Roger went in search, but returned within a short while to say that the whole area was barricaded off by the police, but they had insisted on going through and had seen the charred remains of Alson Twala and Aubrey. They were so badly burnt there was no body to bury.

Two weeks after Aubrey's death an unknown man came to visit Molly, and through him we learnt what happened that day. The man said he was a final year student at university. He said he was part of the huge crowd witnessing the horror of the assault and the burning of the hearse when a well-dressed young man very politely patted him on the shoulder and said, 'Excuse me, would you let me pass through.' He stood aside for this young man, who was Aubrey, and then witnessed my son-in-law raise his arms above his head and say, 'Peace, peace, gentlemen, please don't kill this old man.' To his horror he witnessed the first stab under Aubrey's armpit. He says that he cannot forget that day. He is now unable to concentrate to study, because the vision which will not leave his head is of giving way to this polite, well-dressed young man so that he could go to his death that day.

At the time of Aubrey's murder I was working closely with Sheena Duncan and a committee on the 'Save the Sharpeville Six Campaign', to fight against the death penalty. And I must confess that for a brief time I was in a moral conflict. I did not know whether I wanted the death penalty for those who had murdered those innocent people, Aubrey and Alson. Only with time can such a wound heal. But my conclusion was that I wanted those people who committed that atrocity to be brought to justice, but never to be barbarically hanged.

This was my conclusion, and it is one I will hold to. But my concern for the increasing violence among my own people grows daily. It was expressed so well by a journalist writing for the *Sowetan* on 8 March 1988, four days after Aubrey's death:

> Dammit. We have to stop passing the buck. Something is happening in our community and instead of trying to come to grips with it, we continue to find the usual scapegoat, apartheid. We are eating into ourselves; all respect for human life is gone.
>
> Only the other day it was Maki Skhosana ruthlessly roasted in front of TV cameras. Who can forget that obscene image?
>
> We continue to scream, demanding justice from white South Africa; we continue to protest against detention without trial; we continue demanding democracy. But we also continue to deny ourselves these things.
>
> We refuse to give the other man a hearing.
>
> We continue to be prosecutors, judges and executioners.
>
> And all this turns our struggle for justice into a mockery.

After Aubrey's death Molly just wanted to die. Each event which previously filled her with such joy now only flames her grief. Her birthday is on 20 August, and Aubrey's was on 21 August. They would have a joint birthday celebration. Last year Molly and I shared that sad day together, and we have since sat through a Christmas together.

Her children miss their father deeply. He was a man who would always help them with their homework and take them to school. Molly and her family had to seek some therapeutic help, and Molly, in order to be both mother and provider, has had to postpone her studies for her Master's degree in Communications to work full time.

On 7 February 1989 it was the wedding anniversary of Molly and Aubrey. My grandchildren wrote their mom little notes of comfort, to say:

Strange that happy memories can hurt so much, isn't it? But let's try and make them happy memories and less painfull.
I love you, Mama
from Mpho.

Dear Mama,
Memories should be happy memories. Let them comfort you.
Happy Aniversary
Love
Rirandzu.

We have now completed a one-year cycle of grief at each special event, and perhaps now Molly and her family can renew themselves to face the future without Aubrey.

Molly's last memory of Aubrey is of seeing him in a crowd, and of hearing his words to her that he would be home shortly. She still feels at times as if she catches a glimpse of him in Soweto. Her grief at such moments is unquenchable, and this I can understand, for it catches at a memory of my own.

With my marriage to Tom I gained another daughter, Nomsa, and so there were four daughters in our home. My youngest child was Penny, and her African name was Katura.

Penny was born on 27 March 1954 and grew up to be a very lively young woman, and very active in her small community. She was a member of the YWCA 'Teens' and became their president. At her high school she was treasurer of her school committee. She was not only my daughter but a close friend. We even sang in the church choir together. She shared so many of my aspirations.

Penny was the type of child who, when she moved to a more senior school, would not keep her previous school uniform for her own benefit but would wash and iron it and hand it to her teacher so that another poor child could be given it. One day she came home with a pair of broken shoes and insisted they be taken to the shoe repairer. She explained to me that they were the shoes of an unknown child whom she met in the street and that she had offered to get them repaired and had arranged to meet the child at the same spot next day to return the mended shoes. And once she brought home a young man who was at her high school. He was her senior and like a big brother to her. She had learnt that he was unable to pay his matriculation examination entrance fee and she asked me to provide the money. When I responded that I myself as a single parent bringing up my family could not really afford to pay this fee, she challenged me by saying, 'I know you have a little money saved, may I go and fetch it?' I responded, 'But Penny, it is my only money,' but she replied, 'You always taught me that your God will provide for you.' Naturally I handed the money over to Penny for the young man, who today is a doctor.

On the evening of 15 June 1971 I was returning home to Soweto from work in the city of Johannesburg. I was travelling in a crowded combi taxi, which transports black people from the city back to Soweto. I was seated in the front, and when I looked up I saw my Penny at a taxi rank, chatting and laughing with a group of friends. She wore a blue dress. She did not see me. I knew that she was planning to see her father on that day, who was himself running a taxi service. She was going to see him because she needed his assistance in obtaining a pass-book which she now required. I found my eyes riveted on my lovely daughter, and as we drove past I continued to gaze at her in the rear-view mirror as she became smaller and smaller, fading from my eyes until I could see her no more. And indeed I never saw her alive again. I never saw her dead either, as my family sought to protect me from the image of her death.

Penny was seventeen years old when her life was cut violently and tragically short in a situation which is not in my power to describe. There was terrible pain and devastation to believe that her young life was wasted, but in that loss it was of great importance to me that she should be laid to rest the same way in which she had lived, from the church she had served so well, and where I believe her shining spirit still lives on. I did not want just a cold piece of marble for her tombstone, so the family dedicated four rows of pews in Holy Cross Church, Soweto, in her memory, for the church choir in which she sang in her beautiful soprano voice. Some years later, Dudu placed a marble stone on Penny's grave, which she paid for in instalments with her first wage packet.

Hundreds of Penny's school friends came to the service, and many spoke there. I was strengthened by their love for Penny, and proud also when they talked about her dedication and her work for her school. I can clearly remember one speaker saying that Penny was the kind of treasurer at school who when fund-raising for a project could talk you into putting your hand into your pocket and handing over your last cent, and that no one could resist her passionate appeals; you just had to give. Two of her former girlfriends from that school have now named their children after my Penny.

I think one of the proudest days of my life was at a large meeting in Soweto when all the presidents of different organisations were asked to come forward to stand on the stage and Penny rose to the platform as president of the YWCA Teens, while I remained in the audience as a mere trade unionist.

13

Justice and Reconciliation?

Among the delegates present at the meeting of the Eminent Persons Group in 1986 which I attended was Sheena Duncan, who was at that time President of the Black Sash.[1] At the end of the meeting she approached me to say that she had read in the newspaper that I was now retiring from the union, and she wanted to know what my qualifications were. I told her with pride that I am a self-made person with very little and low qualifications, as I had left school at the age of fourteen years, without completing my Junior Certificate, after my parents divorced and our home was broken. Sheena told me then that the Anglican Church requires the minimum of a Matric pass of its employees, but that in spite of my low educational level she urged me to apply for a vacancy in the Department of Justice and Reconciliation.

Although one of my major fights on behalf of CCAWUSA workers was for pension rights, especially for women, I failed to negotiate any pension for myself. I needed to find another job, and this should have seemed a great opportunity, but because of my non-

[1] The Black Sash was founded (originally as the Women's Defence of the Constitution League) by white women in 1955 to protest over the Nationalist regime's proposal to enlarge the Senate and thus secure the two-thirds majority necessary for taking coloured voters off the common voters' roll. The organisation adopted as its emblem a black ribbon, and its members wore black sashes in public demonstrations to mourn the abrogation of the South African Constitution by the Nationalists. In 1981 it supported a resolution not to rest 'until we have established a democratic South Africa based on the Freedom Charter' and it is at present working to abolish the death penalty in SA.

qualifications I did not do anything about it until Sheena phoned me and insisted that I should. I will always be grateful to Sheena for her faith in me.

I was awarded the post, to my great surprise, and before my appointment was officially announced Sheena distributed a circular to members of the board which touched me. She said:

Dear friends,

It is lovely to be able to write to you with good news for a change.

We have a director for the department [of Justice and Reconciliation].

She is Emma Thandi Mashinini and you will all meet her at APM. She starts with us in July and will be spending June in the US where one of her daughters is graduating.

The Bishops have approved. The Archbishop has interviewed her at length and given his wholehearted approval.

I attach a copy of her CV for your information. It does not convey the dynamism of this pint-sized person. We are exceedingly lucky. She will shake us all up.

Her appointment will be made public after all the technical details are finalised, but the Chairman has said I can tell you all now . . .

My work as Director of the Department of Justice and Reconciliation is to guide and co-ordinate all resource persons in the eighteen dioceses of the Province, consisting of South Africa, Namibia, Swaziland, Lesotho, Mozambique and St Helena, in the Indian Ocean.

One of the very important challenges in my new job is working with detainees. I am part of a task force which draws up a register of detainees and political prisoners, and I suppose it is because I have served many months in detention that I am so acutely aware of the plight of detainees since the State of Emergency. Many people, especially our young people, have been detained, without a crime necessarily having been committed, and they are often subjected to violence and abuse. In the absence of detailed official figures, the DPSC keeps the most comprehensive records available to the public. In 1986 the DPSC knew about the detention of 2840 people under security laws. The police later revealed that 4132 had been detained under security laws that year.

One of the shocking revelations made by the DPSC was the detention of school pupils, some of whom were as young as eleven years old. The children's consciousness of the discriminatory laws, and of the harsh security measures used by the government to suppress their requests for change, has led to an inevitable clash between the victims and the enforcers of the laws. A very popular campaign, Free the Children Alliance, was very active in highlighting the plight of children in detention. It is a crying shame to see children who are ten years old relating their nasty experiences while in detention. I grieve when I think of them as fathers and mothers of tomorrow; what are they going to tell and teach their children? The two predominating effects of detention, say social workers who have observed the results in children who have been released, are depression and anxiety, resulting in loss of interest in life, a loss of esteem, terror, sleeplessness, nightmares, lack of trust and serious medical problems. Some of these effects could last a lifetime.

I notice that their methods with detainees have changed, and I can, even despite all the terrible feelings I suffer because of my detention, count myself lucky to have been able to pick up my life and try to go on with it. The dying in detention seems not to be growing rapidly, as it was, but the people who come out from there are literally vegetables.[1] The methods of torturing people are different.

They are also developing another way of damaging us more. You can see the trend – first it is trade unionists, then it is one-time students. Now – after the restriction on other organisations speaking against apartheid, which society used as their windows for ventilating their oppression and suppression – it is the Church which has emerged to speak on behalf of the people. They never used to detain so many people who work for the Church.[2]

---

[1] During the 25 years of detention without trial there have been 67 deaths in detention, an average of almost three a year. In 1970 and 1972-5 no deaths were recorded; peaks occurred in 1969, with seven deaths, 1976, with thirteen, 1977, thirteen, and 1986, four (Human Rights Commission, Fact Paper 1 (1988): *Detention Without Trial*).

[2] The main target groups for detention without trial are as follows: those working in education; in the Church; as actors, writers and poets; doctors, nurses and social

Another ingredient of South African society is the very high numbers of people killed with capital punishment, a means of retribution I can nowhere find it in my heart to condone, however bad the crime committed, or said to have been committed. On 26 February 1988 the *South African Barometer* published the figures for executions in South Africa since 1977. They are as follows:

1977	93	1983	93
1978	132	1984	131
1979	138	1985	161
1980	132	1986	128
1981	100	1987	164
1982	107		

In 1988 (up to 5 January 1989) 213 death sentences were pronounced, 117 people executed, 48 reprieved and 27 appeals against the death sentence were successful. The South African figures for capital punishment are among the worst in the world.[1]

They kill them seven at a time. And the sorest part of it is that the black families do not believe that their people have been executed, because they cannot see the bodies. It is an absolute African

workers; lawyers; those working in the media; civil servants, members of homeland 'parliaments', party leaders and candidates; and trade union leaders, organisers, shop stewards and workers.

[1] South Africa has the highest execution rate in the world, according to the Centre for Applied Legal Studies (CALS). In the United States, for example, where the number of executions is growing rapidly, it remains less than a third of that of South Africa. In the first three months of 1988 forty-four people were executed at Pretoria Central, compared with three in the United States. The US population is nine times that of South Africa (excluding the 'independent homelands'). In 1987 South Africa executed more people than China, according to CALS.

In the five years from 1983 to 1987 there were 627 executions in South Africa (excluding the 'independent homelands'); in Britain 632 people were hanged over a period of fifty years before the abolition of the death penalty. According to CALS there have been no executions in Western Europe or Australia since 1985. Four years ago Australia became the 28th country to abolish the death penalty.

The South African total for executions in 1986 was 164 people, four times that of Iran, which has a population of about 48 million.

On 5 May 1988 274 people were awaiting execution on Death Row.

Of the 164 people hanged in 1987, 155 were black (102 Africans and 53 Coloureds). Nine were white.

tradition to see the bodies of the dead. We pay our last respects by seeing the body. If you don't see the body inside the coffin, then how do you know what is in that coffin? People could just be removed. Who knows what could have happened to them?

It is very bad for the mothers, not to see the body. The grief at never knowing what is in that coffin, of not being able to see for the last time a child of yours, is just horrible. Terrible grief. I remember I was in Pretoria when Solomon Mahlangu was executed. Immediately after that execution we women from Soweto went and wanted to be with his mother, and when we got there they didn't even give her that sealed coffin or her child to be buried. This body was chased all over, from one cemetery to another, but never was there access to it. And all we could do to sustain her was to share her anger. To identify the solidarity and to share her anger. And at every memorial service of an executed person all the mothers of those who have been executed come to that service and give support to the one whose child has been executed. All the mothers know one another, and have met, and can link together, so your problem is never your problem alone, you are never an island in your problem, and the divisions the government has been trying to create, they are all gone. We unite, and especially we unite in our crisis times.

The thing that is so strange, so remarkable, is that the mothers who are allowed to go to Death Row to see the person who is going to be executed (which is not always the case, by any means) all say – and, you know, it is something which one can't believe – that their children ask, 'Please, don't worry about me. I'm ready to go.' Or, 'Don't cry – I'm going to another country. I am going to be happy.' Like those two women when I was in prison, and I could overhear them talking sweetly to say, 'I must be beautiful to meet my Creator,' and the only angry words they exchanged were about my food, which was standing outside the door and was cold. I only heard of one person who was going to be executed and would not leave his cell. He held on and would not leave, so in the end they put in tear-smokes to get him out. And there is one pastor who is working with the people on Death Row who says it is better to speak with the people on Death Row than with their families, although I myself have always found the families so full of courage, so strong, and I have often felt closer to breaking down than they are.

I have heard white liberals say, 'The black children are throwing their lives away thinking that liberation is just round the corner. And it's not round the corner. The South African government could hold on for five, ten, fifteen years.' And this is so. But this is still only a delay of what will happen. It's just delaying tactics, so that more of us will die. And our black children, they are not afraid to die. None of them. They are prepared to die now. I have heard young girls speaking and saying, 'I definitely am not afraid to die. Because many children have been killed in South Africa. And many are in detention because of fighting for the struggle. So why should we question which child should die and which child should be arrested when all of us are fighting for the same cause?' And I have heard of a boy who said, 'I'm not afraid to die now, but when Mandela's released, *then* I'll be afraid to die.'

The youth are prepared to die now, but they are not prepared to die when liberation comes. And I have been afraid to die, but when liberation is achieved, then, I must say, I am prepared. I've lived a hard life, in many ways a horrible life, but I have always wanted to see the day of liberation. And when we get there, as a coward, perhaps, I am prepared to die, to say: I've lived and struggled for all these years. Now that we've achieved justice – now that we've attained that – now may I not rest in peace?

Appendix A
The South African Trade Union Movement

Almost from the beginning, black workers have been systematically excluded from trade union rights in South Africa.

The first trade unions were formed in the late nineteenth century, mainly by skilled workers from Britain who had emigrated to avoid unemployment at home. So the first unions were craft unions, in the printing and construction industries, for instance, and their members were white, and sometimes Coloured or Malay. Blacks (Africans), when they did enter the labour market, came to agriculture and to the mines, as unskilled workers.

On the mines, they soon came up against competition from unskilled white workers, who saw the migrant workers as threatening their living standards. The whites had the vote, the blacks did not. Hence the birth of an alliance between the majority of white workers and government which was to haunt the development of trade unionism in South Africa: the alliance was based on the concept of so-called 'civilised labour'. So in 1924, the first Industrial Conciliation Act recognised the right of 'employees' to form and join trade unions, to negotiate rates of pay and conditions of work and to withdraw their labour. But it specifically excluded 'pass-bearing natives' (blacks) from the definition of 'employee'. At a stroke, black South Africans were excluded from effective bargaining rights, and most importantly from the right to strike. Black workers were not recognised as 'employees' until 1979.

Black workers did, however, continue to organise. During the 1920s, the Industrial and Commercial Workers' Union (ICU) emerged as a vast and militant general workers' union, with membership drawn from all races (blacks in the majority) and estimated at its height at 100,000. But the Industrial Conciliation Act, combined with differences among the leadership culminating in the expulsion of members of the Communist Party, led to the ICU's eventual decline, and by 1930 it had virtually disintegrated. Separate industrial unions of black workers began to form the basis of a new movement during the 1930s, and in 1941 these unions joined together to form the Council of Non-European Trade Unions (CNETU), which eventually gave way to the South African Congress of Trade Unions (SACTU).

Most of these unions were 'unregistered' under the Industrial Conciliation Act so that they could maintain a black or mixed race membership. Others, such as the Food and Canning Workers' Union, set up a parallel black union for black workers, which shared offices, resources and planning.

In the early 1940s a key organising effort was made by the African National Congress to form an African Mineworkers' Union. And in 1946 the miners went on strike – for a minimum wage of ten shillings (50p) a day. It was a heroic act, for the workers had ranged against them the all-powerful Chamber of Mines, backed by a government which forty years before had been ready to use guns against white miners; and they had little prospect of solidarity from the white miners' union, which was concerned first of all to protect the enormous pay differential between black and white workers. Yet 75,000 black workers took part. Twelve workers were killed in the brutal suppression that followed, and it was over thirty years before there was a union of black mineworkers in South Africa again.

Following the 'election' of the Afrikaner National government in 1948, more racist legislation constrained the black and mixed-race trade unions: in 1953 the Native Labour (Settlement of Disputes) Act established an all-white Bantu Labour Board to replace the system of elected works committees at factory level which had negotiated with employers on behalf of workers. The 1956 Industrial Conciliation Act banned racially mixed unions, forced existing 'mixed' unions to establish separate branches for Asian and Coloured workers, and banned members of these segregated branches from membership of and attendance at executive committee meetings.

In 1954 a so-called Job Reservation Act provided for certain occupations to be 'reserved' for white (and sometimes Coloured or Asian) workers. These measures, combined with the Suppression of Communism Act of 1950, which gave the government extraordinarily wide powers (to ban individuals from office in or membership of certain organisations, from attendance at meetings, from appearing on the premises of newspapers or educational or political or trade union organisations – including in some cases their own work places), put unbearable constraints on trade union organisation. Though SACTU, which remained the principal trade union centre for black workers, was never itself banned (the ANC was declared illegal in 1960, and legal public activity on behalf of the Congress Alliance virtually came to an end), black trade unions went through a hard period for the next twenty years. Their officials were banned, detained, sent into exile.

Through the 1970s, however, unions of black workers began to emerge. Some of them were spontaneous products of shop floor activity; some had support from church or trade union organisations abroad. All were part of a ferment of popular struggle, evidence of that remarkable capacity of an oppressed people to evolve ever new forms and instruments of struggle in the face of suppression.

The Commercial, Catering and Allied Workers' Union of South Africa (CCAWUSA), the union that Emma Mashinini played such a crucial part in building, was part of this ferment, and of the campaign for recognition of African unions which culminated in the recommendation from the government's Wiehahn Commission that employees' rights should be restored to black workers. CCAWUSA in turn played a key role in the formation of the Congress of South African Trade Unions (COSATU), which for five years had a membership of over 600,000 workers, the largest trade union federation in the history of South Africa. It too was restricted under the 'Emergency' laws in 1988, its leaders banned or detained. But the movement built up in those years will not be easy to suppress.

Appendix B

Minutes of Meeting
between
Delegation from Detainees' Parents Support Committee
and
Colonel H. Muller of Security Police

Time: 2.00 pm Thursday, 10 December, 1981.
Venue: 9th Floor, John Vorster Square.
Members of Delegation:

>Mrs. K. Naidoo
>Mrs. P. [Barbara] Hogan
>Mr. T. Mashinini
>Dr. H. J. Koornhoff
>Dr. I. M. Cachalia
>Dr. M. Coleman

Matters Discussed
The Delegation at the start of the meeting and during the course of the meeting emphasised that the meeting had been requested for the purpose of securing equal treatment for all detainees and for all parents and spouses of detainees, and the members of the Delegation had not come to make requests specifically for their own relatives but rather for all detainees.

(1) **ACCEPTANCE OF FOOD PARCELS**
    The Delegation requested that food parcels be accepted for all

detainees without discrimination. Colonel Muller agreed to this, asking that the following be observed:

(a)   Parcels to be brought only on a Friday morning. Exceptions to this day would be considered on representation to Col. Muller, should Fridays be problematical for out-of-town relatives.

(b)   Food parcels not to include perishables, such as sandwiches, cooked meals, etc., but should rather consist of packaged items such as biscuits, chocolates, nuts, fruit juice in cartons, and could include fruit (not too ripe), biltong, dried wors, etc.

(c)   No glass or metal containers.

(d)   Parcel to bear the name of the detainee, and the relative from whom it is sent.

(e)   Each detainee to receive food parcels from one person only each week, this person to be a close relative, or a friend in the case where the close relatives are living elsewhere or for some reason are unable to deliver the parcel.

(f)   Delivery point in all cases to be in the basement of John Vorster Square.

Col. Muller gave the assurance that in those cases where detainees are housed in cells other than at John Vorster Square, the parcels would be promptly distributed to the appropriate police station and that there would be no refusal or delay on the part of the relevant Station Commander in the passing on of the parcel to the detainee. It was pointed out, as an example, that Robert Adam, detained in Pretoria, had received no parcels for three weeks. Col. Muller undertook to investigate this instance.

The Delegation expressed its satisfaction with the above arrangements, but asked that relatives be shown each week the signatures of the detainees to the effect that they had personally received the previous week's parcels. Col. Muller agreed to institute this procedure.

(2)   **ACCEPTANCE OF CLOTHING PARCELS**

It was agreed that exactly the same delivery arrangements for clothing parcels would apply as for food parcels.

Col. Muller agreed that every detainee should be permitted to receive a pillow from his or her relative.

(3) **RETURN OF DIRTY WASHING**
Dirty washing to be collected every Friday morning from John Vorster Square basement, each and every detainee having the right to a weekly change of clothing.

(4) **CHRISTMAS ARRANGEMENTS**
The Delegation made the request that each detainee be permitted a visit close to Christmas Day from parents or spouse. Col. Muller agreed to place the request before the Commissioner of Police and furthermore to recommend its acceptance.
Col. Muller also agreed to detainees receiving up to six Christmas cards from relatives and friends and also to detainees being supplied with up to six cards for them to send to relatives and friends. Messages should be limited to Season's Greetings.
Christmas gifts for detainees will be accepted, subject to Col. Muller's approval of the articles concerned.

(5) **BOOKS, GAMES, PUZZLES**
Each detainee will be permitted to receive books, games or puzzles, but at a time to be approved by Col. Muller. Reading material to be submitted to Col. Muller for acceptance.

(6) **STUDY FACILITIES**
All student detainees will be permitted study material on submission of a study programme or assignments from the detainee's tutors to Col. Muller. Again timing and content is subject to Col. Muller's approval.

(7) **MEDICAL ATTENTION**
It is understood that every detainee is medically examined by the District Surgeon immediately upon detention. Thereafter medical attention is at the request of the detainee. Parents and spouses of detainees are invited to point out any chronic or current ailments of which the detaining authorities should be aware.

(8) **DETAINEES' RIGHTS UNDER SECTION 6**
Subsection (2) of Section 6 of the Terrorism Act states that the Commissioner shall furnish the Minister once a month with reasons why any detainee shall not be released. Col. Muller

confirmed that this requirement is being complied with for each and every detainee within his jurisdiction.

Subsection (3) states that any detainee may at any time make representations in writing to the Minister relating to his detention or release. The Delegation enquired from Col. Muller as to whether every detainee was made aware of this right and whether writing material would be made available to any detainee wishing to exercise this right. Col. Muller stated that there was a definite instruction that this be done and undertook to check on whether this instruction was being carried out in all cases.

Subsection (7) states that a detainee shall be visited in private by a magistrate at least once a fortnight. The Delegation enquired as to whether all detainees were receiving such visits. Col. Muller replied that responsibility for such visits did not lie with the Security Police, but with the Chief Magistrate under instructions from the Minister. All that the Security Police had to do was provide access to the detainees, and as far as he, Col. Muller, was aware, regular visits by magistrates were, in fact, made to all detainees.